The Third Millennium
The Triumph of Our Lady

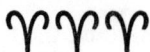

ϒ ϒ ϒ

By
Rev. Msgr. Richard L. Carroll

The Author

Rev. Msgr. Richard L. Carroll has been the Pastor of St. Margaret Mary, Slidell, Louisiana, since January 17, 1970. He is the author of *A Priest Looks at Medjugorje* and *The Remnant Church*. His brother Rev. Msgr. Ralph Carroll is Pastor of St. Clement of Rome in Metairie, Louisiana. They have a sister, Yvonne Hymel who is married to Anthony Hymel. The Hymel's have five children who are all married. Father Carroll's parents are the late Ralph Carroll, Sr. and Myrlie Gremillion Carroll.

FIRST EDITION
10,000 copies

Printed by Book Crafters
Chelsea, Michigan

Manufactured in the United States of American
ISBN # 0-9643572-1-6

Library of Congress Catalog Card No: 96-096892

Copies of this book may be obtained from:
St. Margaret Mary Church
The Third Millennium -- The Triumph of Our Lady
1050B Robert Blvd.
Slidell, Louisiana 70458
Fax: (504) 643-6126

TABLE OF CONTENTS
The Third Millennium
The Triumph of Our Lady

ENTRUSTMENT

This small work is entrusted to Our Lady of Guadalupe, also called Our Lady of the Americas. It was "Our Lady of Guadalupe:" who said "Am I not here who am your mother? Are you not under my shadow and protection? Am I not your fountain of life? Are you not in the folds of my mantle in the crossing of my arms? Is there anything that you need?" (Dec. 12, 1531 - Our Lady to Juan Diego)

Remember, O most gracious Virgin Mary, that never was it known that anyone who fled to thy protection, implored thy help or sought thy intercession, was left unaided. Inspired with this confidence, I fly unto thee, O Virgin of Virgins, my Mother. To thee do I come; before thee I stand sinful and sorrowful. O Mother of the Word Incarnate, despise not my petitions, but in thy mercy hear and answer them.
Amen.

The Council of Ephesus in 430 AD called her the "Mother of God." I have come to know her as my mother. It is to her that I humbly dedicate this work to be used by her as she wishes. To Jesus through Mary! Totus Tuus -- Totally Yours!

INTRODUCTION
Preparing for the Third Millennium

I was invited by the IHS Network in Rosemont, Pennsylvania, to give a talk at a Catholic Unity Conference on June 23, 1996. The title of the talk was "A Parish United." This conference was held at the Ramada Inn in Essington, PA. near the international airport serving Philadelphia.

As I was preparing this talk, I realized that our Holy Father has written a prophetic document on the "Coming of the Third Millennium." I then felt a need to consider writing a book as a follow up to *The Remnant Church*. It is clear that a new era in the Church is soon to begin.

I believe the message given to Father Gobbi on December 5, 1994. Our Lady tells her "beloved priests" that the Triumph of the Immaculate Heart of Mary will occur by the year 2000. This means that we may expect the tribulations predicted in the Book of Revelation to occur soon.

Our Lady told Father Gobbi, "I confirm to you that, by the Great Jubilee of the year two thousand, there will take place the Triumph of my Immaculate Heart, of which I foretold you at Fatima, and this will come to pass with the return of Jesus in glory to establish his reign in the world. Then you will at last be able to see with your own eyes the new heavens and the new earth."[1] This message was received by Father Gobbi at the shrine of Our Lady of Guadalupe, Mexico City on December 5, 1994.

These are "private revelations," and no one is bound to accept them. The great danger is that so many parishes will be so poorly prepared, if Our Lady truly is trying to warn us. I certainly recognize that many of our parishes are being led by the Holy Spirit to prepare for the third millennium, regardless of whether Our Lady's messages to Fr. Gobbi are authentic or not.

Synopsis of the Book

The first question that comes to mind in reviewing a book is, "Why did the author write this book?"

After reading the Holy Father's encyclical I felt drawn to share the dream I have for St. Margaret Mary Parish: **to be prepared for the fulfillment of Our Lady's promise at Fatima, the Triumph of the Immaculate Heart of Mary**. If we see ourselves as children, it is easy to imagine the promise of Mary could take place in our lifetime. At the same time, I realized that even if the return of Jesus Christ does not occur at least I will be able to say that our community is ready for the third millennium.

Scripture tells us, "...your young men shall see visions and your old men will dream dreams."(Acts 2:17) Many of the young in this parish have seen extraordinary signs. It seems much harder for the old to dream dreams. Many of our clergy who have born the heat of the day are burned out. Many of the programs presented to us in the past seemed to require more and more from our priests, and we never seemed to measure up.

During the serious health problems I have encountered in the past three years, Our Blessed Mother has placed on my heart a simple message to her beloved priests sons, "As long as she (Mary) is near you, you have nothing to fear." This small book is meant primarily for Our Lady's priest-sons to allay any fear. Mary is at your side.

CBS had an example of what this panic will be like as we approach the year 2000. A fundamentalist sect in Columbia recently convinced the people that June 6th, 1996 was 666, the day of the Devil. "Any child not baptized will be snatched away by Satan," they were told. Pandemonium reigned!

Many believe that the end of the world is near. Our Lady's message is clear: "you have nothing to fear as long as Our Blessed Mother is beside you." We look forward to the "Triumph of the Immaculate Heart of Mary," for this will usher in an "era of peace" and not the end of the world.

The Goals of *Tertio Millennio Adveniente*[2]

As I read the Holy Father's letter on the third millennium, it seems to me to set our three goals:

1.   Eucharistic - in the year 2000 there will be a Eucharistic congress in Rome. The return of Jesus Christ could be by our belief in the real presence of Jesus in the Eucharist. Today, according to the gallup poll, only 30% of American Catholics believe what the church teaches - (that Jesus Christ is truly present Body and Blood, Soul and Divinity in the Eucharist.) Each Catholic parish must develop a great love for Jesus Christ in the Eucharist.

Sister Briege McKenna tells of a major seminary in our country in which the spiritual director wanted to encourage devotion to the Blessed Sacrament. Instead of a talk, he asked the major seminarians to spend an hour in adoration before the Blessed Sacrament. Their response was: "We are not bread watchers." Do you wonder why 70% of American Catholics don't believe in the "real presence of Jesus in the Eucharist?"

2.   The second goal the Holy Father sets before us is Unity. It is his dream that the prayer of Jesus would be answered "that all may be one"(John 17:21). This union would take place within the One, Holy Catholic and Apostolic Church.

3.   The final goal is also a prayer of Jesus: "that **the will of God the Father be done of Earth as it is in Heaven**," as found in the prayer we call "The Our Father."

The Role of Our Lady

When we speak about the triumph of the Immaculate Heart of Mary, it is a **triumph of intercession**. Sacred Scripture gives us a wonderful example of the Triumph of the Immaculate Heart of Mary. In the Book of Esther in the Old Testament, King Ahasuerus of Persia had decided to annihilate the Jewish people on the thirteenth day of the month. Queen Esther interceded before the king to save the Jewish people. Our Blessed Mother intercedes before her son, Jesus, to prevent the destruction of the world. Because of Mary's intercession Jesus will grant us His **Divine Mercy**, just as King Ahasuerus did for Queen Esther. As a result of Mary's intervention, we will be given an era of peace. This will result in the Triumph of the Immaculate Heart of Mary and the return of Jesus Christ as Eucharistic Lord.[3]

The Triumph of the Immaculate Heart of Mary, the prevention of world annihilation and Mary's promised period of peace began with the Holy Father's collegial consecration of the world to her Immaculate Heart on March 25, 1984. It is our hope that this Triumph will be fulfilled in the near future.

How Can These Goals be Accomplished?

The Holy Father, Pope John Paul, II, answered very simply: "**only by the Holy Spirit**." We won't change hearts through pastoral programs. However, there are some things we can do. The Holy Father tells us as a remote preparation we need conversion.

In the book, *The Remnant Church* you are shown some of the ways we tried to bring about this conversion at St. Margaret Mary. It started with Perpetual Adoration in 1983 and hundreds have committed themselves to love of Jesus present in the Eucharist.

St. Margaret Mary Parish has been consecrated to the Immaculate Heart of Mary and the Sacred Heart of Jesus. Hundreds made the Act of Total Consecration of St. Louis de Monfort on March 25, 1994. This has become a yearly devotion. All of our children are enrolled in the scapular of Our Lady at First Holy Communion and free scapulars are available in the chapel. First Saturday devotions are encouraged. Every class in our school has a Cenacle of prayer once a week. The children say the rosary, praise and worship God in song, and learn from about 50 prayer Moms to become intercessors. I believe my recovery from life threatening surgery last October was due in great measure to the prayers of these children.

The Holy Spirit has become a great force in this parish. Our 8th graders and High School Seniors participate in "Life in the Spirit" retreats put on by college students and priests.

The Three Important Ways to Prepare

There are three things that St. Margaret Mary Parish does that I believe will help our community to be prepared for the third millennium. All three of these may not be practical in many parishes. At least pastors could encourage their parishioners to participate in the communities that furnish them.

1.   Divine Mercy
Divine Mercy involves the Sacrament of Penance and the healing of shame through masses of inner healing

and generational healing. Each shepherd must bring his flock back to this most important sacrament.

2.   Discipleship
       To become a disciple, you must accept Jesus as Lord and Savior. A disciple must do what the Lord tells you to do. We know this through prayer, study of Sacred Scripture and learning the teachings of the Church. As a disciple of Jesus Christ, we have a longing to bring others into the Church. Hence, evangelization springs from our attempts to become "fully armed disciple of Jesus Christ."

3.   Intercessory Prayer
       The final thing we do that I would recommend is intercessory prayer. A small core group meets at 6:15 p.m. The rosary is recited at 7:00 p.m. We have praise and worship music from 7:30 to 8:00 p.m. A time of intercessory prayer for the universal church as well as individual testimonies follow. Mass begins at 9:00 p.m.

       Once a month on the first Friday we have a Mass of Inner Healing and anointing of those who wish. We have lay prayer teams trained by Fr. Joe Benson and Sister Veronica that pray over anyone who desires prayers after every Friday Night Intercessory Prayer Meeting. The three parish priests are involved in the healing ministry.

Conclusion -- Totus Tuus

       In our community we have shared the love of the priests for our Holy Father, Pope John Paul, II. We have supported our own Archbishop Francis Schulte in obedience and love. I am personally indebted to our Ordinary, Archbishop Schulte, for his constant support of me during my three years of illness. Priests today from the Pope to the lowliest curate are "victim souls."

Both our Holy Father and our own archbishop have pointed the way to the third millennium by their love of Our Blessed Mother. This book gives me an opportunity to share with my brother priests what the Holy Spirit is doing to help us prepare for the third millennium. I have been blessed with two outstanding pastoral associates. Fr. Mossy Gallagher, a 73 year old priest from Ireland, ministers to the sick and elderly primarily in Slidell Memorial Hospital. Fr. Joe Benson is also from Ireland. His personal testimony in this book will be a tremendous gift to anyone burdened by shame. Father Benson also assisted me in understanding discernment, based on years of Spiritual direction to countless souls.

Knowing Our Blessed Mother is by the side of each of my brother priests, I beg Our Lady to intercede for each of you. May she share with each of you, as she has with me, a message of hope. "As long as I am near you, you have nothing to fear."

ACKNOWLEDGMENTS

This book is written with the hope of reaching the hearts of as many as possible to help you prepare for the third millennium. This will be a time of great anxiety for many who will not know where to turn. The Holy Spirit will tell each of you what you are to do: "Seek the Lord while he may be found..." (Isaiah 55:6)

It is my firm hope that this work will help priests in particular who will be subject to great persecution in the next few years. Our Blessed Mother's message is very simply: "as long as I am near you, you have nothing to fear."

I would like to acknowledge my wonderful staff in the church, school and CCD offices at St. Margaret Mary in Slidell. I would like to recognize Joleen Megilligan, Alice Sanders, Linda Latour and Lori Mire. I am especially grateful to Shannon M. Gallo who did the majority of the typing and editing of this manuscript. Special thanks are due to Patsie Meyer, Pat Dalton, Judy Folmer and Linda Knauer for editing this book.

I am indebted to my two associate pastors Fr. Mossy Gallagher and Fr. Joseph Benson. By prayer and example Fr. Mossy Gallagher helps sustain us. Fr. Joe Benson enriched this work by his incredible testimony and the sharing of his wisdom and discernment learned through years of counseling and offering spiritual direction to countless individuals. Both men are an incredible blessing to me personally.

The front and back cover are done by a young artist and parishioner of St. Margaret Mary Church, Mike Borgatti. Prints may be purchased by writing to:

Mr. Mike Borgatti / St. Margaret Mary Church
1050 Robert Blvd.
Slidell, La. 70458

The etchings throughout the book were done by Ann Michel. Copies can be ordered from:

Mrs. Ann Michel
3923 Hopewood Lane
Winston Salem, N.C. 27103
(910) 766-8843

[1] United States National Headquarters of the Marian Movement of Priests, *Our Lady speaks to her Beloved Priests* (St. Francis, Maine, 1990). Page 893, Number 532.

[*] Please Note: All Biblical quotations in this book come from The New American Bible.

[2] Pope John Paul, II, *Tertio Mellenio Adveniente*, (Boston, MA.: Pauline Books & Media, 1994).

[3] The Bishops' Committee of the Confraternity of Christian Doctrine, *The New American Bible* (Nashville: Thomas Nelson Publishers, 1983), The Book of Esther Chapters 3-5.

Jesus I Trust in You!

BLESSED FAUSTINA

Section One
Divine Mercy

Jesus said to Blessed Faustina: "I have opened my heart as a living fountain of mercy. Let all souls draw life from it"[1]

"Since Abraham, intercession - asking on behalf of another - has been characteristic of a heart attuned to God's mercy. In the age of the Church, Christian intercession participates in Christ's, as an expression of the communion of saints. In intercession, he who prays looks, 'not only to his own interests, but also to the interests of others,' even to the point of praying for those who do him harm"[2]
(Catechism of the Catholic Church)

Chapter One
Divine Mercy

A key element in the preparation for the Third Millennium and the Triumph of Our Lady is our openness to Divine Mercy. We are living in a time that Jesus is pouring out graces in abundance. This is a manifestation of His Divine Mercy.

We recognize that Divine Mercy will never end. There is concern that the other side of the coin of Divine Mercy is divine justice. Many times Our Lady has spoken to Father Gobbi about holding back the hand of God's justice. Clearly, scripture teaches in the book of Revelation that there will be a period of tribulation which will last approximately three and a half years. If we accept the possibility that these prophecies could occur in the near future, Divine Mercy takes on new significance and a sense of urgency.

History of Devotion to "Divine Mercy"[3]

One of the most powerful weapons in this day to fight Satan is the Divine Mercy of Jesus Christ. In our community, we have begun the devotion to Jesus under the title of Divine Mercy. A brief history of this devotion is important to understand.

Helen Kowalska was born in Poland on August 25, 1905. She attended school for only two years and began work at age 9. At age 7, she knew she wanted to be a nun and at 15, her parents refused to let her enter a convent. On August 1 of 1923, she was at a dance and while there, saw Jesus covered with wounds asking her, "For how long must I support your infidelity to me?" She fled to a church. Our Lord spoke to her saying, "Go to Warsaw and enter a convent."

During Mass in Warsaw, she heard the words, "Go and see this priest. Tell him everything. He will show you what to do." The priest got her a job with a pious family, but she was refused admission to the convent.

Finally, on August 1, 1925, when she was 20, she was accepted as a postulant by the Sisters of Our Lady of Mercy. On April 30, 1928, she made her first vows and five years later, her final vows. Her religious name was Sister Faustina. On May 11, 1936, doctors found she had tuberculosis. She died on October 5, 1938, at the age of 33.

On November 30, 1980, Pope John Paul II wrote his second encyclical entitled, "Rich in Mercy." Sister Faustina was declared "Blessed" by Pope John Paul, II in April 18, 1993. This is the final step before canonization, the process to recognize someone as a "Saint" in the Catholic Church.

The Mission of Sister Faustina

Jesus appeared a number of times to give her this special message:

"To inflame the whole world with complete trust in God's infinite mercy. To bring everyone to the contemplation of the Savior's pierced heart from which flowed blood and water."

The Picture of the Merciful Christ

On February 22, 1931, the Merciful Christ appeared to Sister Faustina for the first time in Plock, Poland. Jesus' right hand was raised in blessing while the left was touching his garment at the breast where two large rays came forth, one red, the other pale. Jesus said, "Paint an image according to the pattern you see with the inscription, 'Jesus, I trust in You.' I promise that the soul that will venerate this image will not perish. I also promise victory over its enemies already here on earth, especially at the hour of death. I, myself, will defend it as my own glory. I am offering people a vessel with which they are to keep coming for graces to the fountain of mercy. That vessel is this image with the inscription, 'Jesus, I trust in You.' I desire that the image be venerated first in your chapel and then throughout the world."

"The two rays denote blood and water. The pale ray stands for the water which makes souls righteous. The red ray stands for the blood which is the life of souls. These two rays issued forth from the depths of My tender mercy when My agonized heart was opened by a lance on the cross. Happy is the one who will dwell in this shelter for the just hand of God shall not lay hold of him."

Another time Jesus said, "By means of this image, I shall grant many graces to souls. It is to be a reminder of the demands of My mercy because even the strongest faith is of no avail without works."

Trust in Divine Mercy

The Redeemer told her:

"My daughter, the fire of my mercy consumes me."

"Lack of confidence breaks my heart. Even more painful for me is the lack of trust in zealous persons."

"I am all love and all mercy, and a soul that trusts in Me is happy, for I, Myself, take care of her. No sin, no matter how sordid will exhaust My mercy, for the more one draws from it the more it increases."

"**I want priests to proclaim My great mercy. I want sinners to come to me without any fear whatever. Even if a soul is like a fully corrupted corpse, even if,**

4

humanly speaking, there is no further remedy, it's not like that before Me. I am more generous with sinners than with the just. It is for them that I shed my Blood. Pray as much as possible for those in their agony. Obtain for them trust in my mercy."

Principal Elements of Devotion to the Divine Mercy

1. Sacrament of Reconciliation -- Penance.
2. Veneration of the picture of Jesus as Divine Mercy.
3. Feast of Divine Mercy, first Sunday after   Easter. "I desire," says the Lord, "that the feast of My mercy be refuge and shelter for all souls, especially for   poor sinners."
4. Chaplet of Divine Mercy. On September   13, 1935, Sister Faustina had a vision of an angel enforcing divine justice, hurling lightening and thunder. A prayer poured out: "Father, I offer You the Body and Blood, Soul and Divinity of Your dearly beloved Son, our Lord Jesus Christ, in atonement for our sins and those of the whole world." The avenging angel   disappeared. The next day she   heard, "Every time you enter the chapel, repeat immediately the prayer I taught you yesterday."

Chaplet of Divine Mercy

Sister Faustina was told that the Chaplet of Divine Mercy is to be said using rosary beads. It is said as follows:

Our Father, Hail Mary, Apostles' Creed - On the large beads say, "Eternal Father, I offer You the Body and Blood, Soul and Divinity, of Your dearly beloved Son, our Lord Jesus Christ, in atonement for our sins and those of the whole world." On the ten small beads say, "For the sake of His sorrowful passion, have mercy on us and on the whole world." In conclusion, say three times, "Holy God, Holy

Mighty One, Holy Immortal One, have mercy on us and on the whole world."

Our Blessed Mother appeared to Sister Faustina with this promise and warning: "Fear nothing, I gave the Savior to the world. You have to speak of His great mercy to prepare the world for His coming again."

In an attempt to encourage devotion to the Divine Mercy at St. Margaret Mary Church, we have placed a picture of the Divine Mercy in our chapel and in the vestibule of the church. We began the recitation of the Divine Mercy Novena, which goes from Good Friday to Divine Mercy Sunday, about three years ago.

Every night prior to the evening Mass, we recite both the Rosary and the Chaplet of Divine Mercy. These are clearly the times to call on Jesus for this gift of Divine Mercy. On the last page of this book, you will find a prayer approved by the Church for the enthronement of the home. One the inside of the back cover you will find a picture of Divine Mercy.

✞✞✞✞✞

Divine Mercy Sunday Sermon
April 14, 1996

Imagine that it is now the year 2006. The children surround the old priest. Once more they ask him to tell them about the "Triumph of the Immaculate Heart of Mary" and how peace came into the world.

"No one would ever believe", Fr. Carroll begins, "that peace was possible." The 20th century was filled with wars, violence in the home through abuse, violence in our streets through seemingly endless murders. Thirty-four million children had been aborted in the United States

alone. This heinous crime was hidden under the subterfuge of 'freedom of choice.'

"Abortion was soon to be followed by euthanasia under the absurd title of 'Right to Die with Dignity'. It seemed as if no crime was too unthinkable for 20th century man.

"The final four years of the last century brought about the greatest change since the first coming of Jesus. This period would usher in the return of Jesus Christ; it would be highlighted by the Triumph of the Immaculate Heart of Mary.

"Our Blessed Mother had promised the three children in Fatima that the Triumph of her Immaculate Heart was part of God the Father's plan, In 1917 Mary predicted the end of World War I and the beginning of the Second World War. She foretold the rise of communism in Russia and its ultimate defeat. Mary spoke of her triumph, not as the end of the world, but the beginning of a great era of peace. Perhaps Jesus' prayer to God the Father would be finally realized; namely, that God the Father's will would be done here 'on earth as it is in heaven.'

"On Mercy Sunday, April 14, 1996, I knew that the Triumph was near. Sister Faustina, a young nun in Poland had been given the task by Jesus to foster devotion to the Divine Mercy. Yet she died in 1938 at the age of 33.

"Her task was picked up by Cardinal Wojtyla who would become Pope John Paul II. His second encyclical was entitled 'Rich in Mercy'. Pope John Paul II put everything in place to complete Sister Faustina's mission. As a cardinal he was instrumental in lifting the Vatican ban on devotion to Jesus under the title of 'Divine Mercy'. As pope, he allowed the Sunday after Easter to be celebrated

as Divine Mercy Sunday. The novena and the Litany of Divine Mercy were now being said by countless Catholics.

"The skies over Slidell, Louisiana were cloudy on April 14, 1996. That night there was a deluge of rain and hail. It was as if Our Lady herself were confirming the events soon to take place.

Prophecy of St. John Bosco

"St. John Bosco had predicted that the Pope of the end times would be wounded, recover, and then be killed. Pope John Paul II, who is reported to have seen Our Lady, knew he was to be a martyr for the faith.

"In St. John Bosco's vision the Church would be guided by two lights during the great battle. On one pillar stood Our Blessed Mother, the other the Eucharist.

"The prophecies of Malachy, published in the sixteenth century, recorded only two popes to follow John Paul II. The first was called "De Gloria Olivae", the glory of the olive tree. This could indicate either great suffering or possibly the antichrist. The final pope of the end times was called by Malachy, 'Petrus Romanus' - Peter of Rome. As you know, the first leader of the apostles, or popes, was Peter, who suffered crucifixion. No other pope in 20 centuries ever carried the name Pope Peter.

"It is clear from Our Lady's statement at Fatima that this was not to be the end of the world but the end of an era. The Triumph of the Immaculate Heart of Mary would usher in a period of great peace.

"I believe Peter of Rome will bring all Christians together into the one Catholic faith. Jesus Himself had prayed: 'that all may be one as you, Father, are in me, and

I in you;" (John 17:21) At this time he will simply be called Peter of Rome, Bishop.

"Divine Mercy has taught all of us a lesson; in God the Father's eyes we are all sinners. When we are given the gift of illumination, we recognized, not only that we were sinners, but that it is Jesus Christ Himself who saves us through his Divine Mercy.

The Illumination or Mini-Judgment

"By Mercy Sunday, 1996, I knew the illuminations, predicted by Our Blessed Mother in Garabandal (1961-1965) and confirmed in the writing of Sister Faustina as well as Fr. Gobbi, were about to occur world-wide. It was clear to me that Divine Mercy would occur when people throughout the world saw themselves as all of us are, sinners in the eyes of God our Father.

"But would there be time for them to repent? Would they even understand what they were going through when they experience this religious phenomenon that I had lived through in 1994? In countless apparitions Our Lady had said: 'My children are so unprepared.'"

Sadly, I awoke from my day dreaming. It was still April, 1996.

The prophecies had not yet been fulfilled. But I knew, beyond a doubt, one more piece in the puzzle of how Our Lady would bring about her triumph. It seemed absolutely too simple to be true. Mary, our Mother, wanted to use the remnant churches to prepare for this awesome event - the return of Jesus Christ, and His final plan was intercessory prayer.

9

Chapter Two
The Sacrament of Penance

"... The joy of every Jubilee is above all a joy based on the forgiveness of sins, the joy of conversion. It therefore seems appropriate to emphasize once more the theme of the Synod of Bishops in 1984: 'penance and reconciliation.'"[4]
(Pope John Paul, II)

"By Christ's will, the church possesses the power to forgive the sins of the baptized and exercises it through bishops and priests normally in the Sacrament of Penance."[5]
(Catechism of the Catholic Church)

✟✟✟✟✟

Preparing for the Third Millennium and The Triumph of Our Lady

In *The Remnant Church*, I detailed the efforts of our community at St. Margaret Mary in Slidell, Louisiana to live the gospel messages. These gospel messages are of penance, prayer and love for Jesus Christ through the Eucharist and devotion of Our Blessed Mother.

This book is a journal of the spiritual growth of a parish. It is an ongoing story of an entire community seeking to make Jesus the Lord of our lives. The Holy Spirit is not finished with us yet. It is my hope that our story would inspire others to be open to the work of the Holy Spirit in their own communities.

In the second edition of *The Remnant Church*, I detailed our efforts to understand the importance of the sacrament of penance. Throughout our country you hear priests and laymen alike saying, "No one is going to confession any longer." Many parishes have as little as fifteen minutes of time devoted to this important sacrament.

A good friend of mine, Dr. George Hogben, tells me that as Catholics have given up on confession, his profession of psychiatry has grown. "For many Catholics," Dr. Hogben says, "psychiatry has replaced the confessional box." "The sad thing," Hogben reports, "is that psychiatry can identify sin, but it cannot forgive sin."

1,200 Adults Come to Confession

On March 15, 1994, 1,200 adults came to St. Margaret Mary to experience the Sacrament of Penance. This is a tremendous number when you realize that only about 2,500 of our parishioners, including children, come to church on Sunday. It all began with a letter I sent to each member of our parish. The letter, dated March 11, 1994, was a summons to repentance.

This will begin to expose my own personal journey into Divine Mercy. It would be one of the most profound events in my life. After reading *Seeking Purity of Heart* by Joseph Breault, which was given to me by Fr. Joe Benson, associate Pastor at St. Margaret Mary, I experienced my own "mini judgment" or "illumination." Sharing the intimacy of a personal religious experience takes an enormous amount of trust in a community. I would not have had the courage to do this if I had not received the grace of being pastor of St. Margaret Mary for nearly twenty-five years.

As you read my personal testimony concerning my "mini judgment," you must be aware of the dangers in this type of sharing of a religious experience.

A prayerful parishioner told me of a vision Our Blessed Mother gave to her. She was combing the hair of one of her beautiful daughters. As she peered into the mirror she was surprised to see my face.

"Tell father," Our Blessed Mother said: "This is what people see when he talks about himself." She looked again into the mirror and saw the face of her pastor, Fr. Carroll.

"But tell father, when he speaks of Jesus, this is what people see," Our Blessed Mother continued. As the parishioner looked again into the mirror she saw a beautiful image of Jesus Christ.

It is therefore my hope that the sharing of this religious experience in 1994 will allow you to see the incredible image of Jesus Christ - as Divine Mercy.

✟✟✟✟

The Initial Letter on Divine Mercy
March 11, 1994

My Dear Parishioners,

In the last few years our community at St. Margaret Mary has received a calling to become a remnant. We have seen the outpouring of the Holy Spirit that resulted from Perpetual Adoration. We have grown spiritually because of the great devotion we have to Our Blessed Mother. We have a reputation far and wide for our loyalty to the Holy Father and the Catholic Church.

I believe the Holy Spirit is now calling us to a more intimate relationship with Jesus Christ as Lord. The next piece of the puzzle for becoming a *Remnant Church* demands a surrender to Jesus as Lord of our lives. Many of you are already planning to make the Act of Total Consecration on March 25, 1994.[6] All our children in St. Margaret Mary School will make this consecration on that day.

Whether you make the Act of Consecration or not, I feel we are being led as a community to make Jesus the Lord of our lives. To do this, we need to prepare ourselves by making a complete confession of our sins. Many of you have already answered this call at our recent mission with Father Straub. Most of you have not gone to confession for years. This must change if the Holy Spirit is to use us in this coming time of chastisement.

Recently, one of our parishioners told me of a private audience held by our Holy Father. The best friend of this parishioner attended this audience and assisted at Mass with three Jesuit priests. The four of them learned that the Pope is regularly seeing Our Blessed Mother. At Mass the Holy Father said, not once, but eight times, "We are living in the end times." I find that statement, coming from a man whom we all admire, awesome.

We know from the approved messages of Fatima, that Our Lady warns of the impending tribulations found in scripture in the Book of Revelation. Mary promises us that in the end, Satan will be defeated. The Immaculate Heart will triumph and world peace achieved.[7]

Jesus warned us through scripture that in the end times, "False prophets will rise in great numbers to mislead many" (Matthew 24:11). Many priests have said that confession is obsolete.

Satan has been able to deceive countless others and myself about the authenticity of visionaries who have failed to get Church approval. Satan is real and his power is now reaching its climax.

One way Satan has deceived countless Catholics has been in the area of the need for confession. Many of you, I know, have not gone to confession because one priest or the other said that, "Very few Catholics commit mortal sin." This is a delusion that has affected even many priests.

There are countless Catholics who regularly miss Sunday Mass, which is objectively a mortal sin, and routinely return the following Sunday to receive communion without going to confession. This is a sacrilege and a grave sin. St. Paul warns us, "... whoever eats the bread or drinks the cup of the Lord unworthily sins against the body and blood of the Lord." (I Corinthians 11:27)

I believe that St. Margaret Mary parish is being led to spiritual intimacy with Jesus Christ as Lord. However, now it's up to you. If you have not gone to confession for a year or more, you need prayerfully to consider doing so. We will have a Penance Service on Tuesday, March 15, 1994, at 7:30 p.m., following the 6:30 p.m. Mass. We will have at least six or seven priests available for confession. You need to come.

On November 13, 1980, our Holy Father, Pope John Paul, II wrote an encyclical entitled, *On the Mercy of God* In this letter the Pope said:

"The church lives an authentic life when she professes and proclaims mercy. The most stupendous attribute of the Creator and of the Redeemer, -- and when she brings people close to the sources of the Savior's mercy, of which she is the trustee and dispenser. Of great significance in this area is constant meditation on the word of God and above all conscious and mature participation in the Eucharist and in the Sacrament of Penance or Reconciliation. It is the sacrament of penance or reconciliation that prepares the way for each individual even those weighed down with great faults. In this sacrament each person can experience mercy in a unique way. That is the love which is more powerful than sin.[8]

14

I believe we are now in the period of Divine Mercy. If you have been away from the Catholic Church for any reason, this is an invitation from Jesus Himself to come home. If Satan has deceived you, as he has many others, you need to understand that Satan's power has never been greater. Monthly confession should not be a luxury for the few, but a habit for the majority. You need to come Tuesday night.

We now know that Satan's favorite target has been priests. Sister Briege McKenna, the nun involved in the healing ministry, was told by Our Lady that priests are Satan's favorite targets. I show the scars of my failures to defeat Satan in my life. I also know that families are Satan's next favorite target. My special plea is for all to come and hear about God's mercy.

When I made the decision that all the priests would speak this weekend on Divine Mercy, I hoped that Scripture would provide us a suitable text. The second reading is from St. Paul's letter to the Ephesians 2:4-8:
"But God is rich in mercy; because of his great love for us he brought us to life with Christ when we were dead in sin. Both with and in Christ Jesus he raised us up and gave us a place in the heavens, that in the ages to come he might display the great wealth of his favor, manifested by his kindness to us in Christ Jesus. I repeat, it is owing to His favor that salvation is yours through faith. This is not your own doing, it is God's gift; ..."

Finally, one of the things that I believe will occur during the time of chastisement is this; we will see ourselves as we really are in God's eyes. Father Joe Benson shared a story with me. As a young priest he was called upon at an international conference of priests to hear the confession of the clergy. An elderly priest came in and demanded to know by what right this youngster had to hear his confession. "You can stay or you can leave," Fr. Joe responded. The priest proceeded to pour out his sins for the next hour and a half. He had not been to confession in more than fifty years. So moved was this elderly priest by his confession that he sent a card of thanks to Fr. Joe. Six months later he died. If Satan can deceive even the priests like this, how much more easily will he deceive the laity.

At the same international conference, Leanne Payne, a pastoral counselor told the priests, "My prayer for you is that you recognize yourselves as you truly are before the Lord." Fr. Joe and others actually witnessed priests jump in shock at what they were experiencing.

My prayer for you, my dearest children, is to keep you under the protective custody of Our Lady. Two different individuals have seen our community in a vision. It was during the coming time of Chastisement and we were under the protective bubble of Our Lady. However, make no mistake about it; **regular confession is a necessary component to secure our place in the Remnant Church.**

If our Divine Savior issues you a call to repentance, I beg you to come Tuesday night, March 15th. You will never regret heeding that summons.

With Deepest Love,
Father Carroll[9]

✝✝✝✝✝

Weekend Sermon
March 11-12, 1994

One day when your grandchildren ask you to tell them a story, gather them close around the fire and tell them the story about the Ark. It wasn't Noah's Ark; it was the Ark that saved us, the church we called the Remnant. The Holy Spirit used the Virgin Mother of God to crush the serpent's head. The Church even called Mary, The Ark of the Covenant.

Father Richard Carroll, was the pastor of St. Margaret Mary Church in Slidell, Louisiana. On March 11, 1994 at 11:00 p.m. he returned from blessing the home of one of his precious daughters who was being subjected to the attack of Satan. She was so fearful of Satan she couldn't sleep in her room. Many people at the time didn't believe in the devil. This pastor knew better.

At 2:15 a.m. Saturday morning, March 12, 1994, he finished his third Rosary and listened to a wonderful tape by Kathleen Keefe from Yonkers, New York, a mother of seven who has a healing ministry to priests.

Although Fr. Carroll had already prepared his homily for Saturday night Our Blessed Mother wouldn't let him sleep. Finally, he gave in and decided to write the final chapter of The Remnant Church.

His parishioners had heard over and over how the Holy Spirit was building a Remnant. Jesus wanted every Catholic parish to be a Remnant. Jesus had warned in scripture, "When the Son of Man comes, will He find any faith on the Earth?" (Luke 18:8) Fr. Carroll was afraid that Christ would find little faith and few remnants.

Building the Ark was the easy part. More than ten years earlier our community had begun Perpetual Adoration of the Blessed Sacrament. Hundreds of parishioners spent an hour a week in adoration of Jesus. The love of Jesus in the Eucharist was phenomenal.

The Holy Spirit showed us the importance of the love of Our Blessed Mother. She confirmed that importance to us through many signs.

A few months earlier someone told him how Mary brought her into the Ark - The Remnant Church. Her baby had died inside her womb. The doctor was going to remove it surgically but first he took an ultrasound. The Protestant, whose name was Dianne, had never prayed to Mary. After all, she was a Protestant. "I don't know why I did it," Dianne said, "but as they were taking the picture, I prayed, Mary save my baby." At that moment, miraculously, the baby turned over in her womb and began sucking her thumb. She was born a healthy child they named Bridget.

Over seven years went by and Dianne never became a Catholic. Last year her Catholic husband convinced Dianne to attend a Charismatic conference in New Orleans. At noon, when others left for lunch they moved close to the front of the hall.

Suddenly a stranger stood before them. "Our Lady wants your daughter to pray before the Tilma," she said. The Tilma is a picture or image of Our Lady of Guadalupe or Our Lady of the Americas. Bridget and her dad obediently got up to pray before the picture of Our Lady.

The stranger said to Dianne, "You asked God for a sign, if you should become Catholic. Jesus said, 'When you prayed to my Mother, she came and asked me to save your child. The sign you wanted is your healthy child,

Bridget.'" That Protestant convert and her family received a ticket to the Ark.

"Wait," the children listening to your story will cry! "What tickets?"

"I will tell you later," the storyteller continued.

Father Carroll learned that to be a Remnant Church, his community had to love the Pope and listen to his authority. That was easy at St. Margaret Mary because they loved Pope John Paul, II.

Our Blessed Mother was telling priests to bring their people back to the sacraments, particularly the Eucharist and Confession. "If you do this," she promised, "the outpouring of Divine Mercy would occur in our Church." Many will get a ticket to the Ark because of this great grace.

The children hearing this story were getting restless. "Tell us about the Chastisement."

"All right," the storyteller went on. Father Carroll now knew that the Ark was near completion. The surprise was how few were ready to take the boat. Everyone had an excuse - after all it was exam week.

In late February 1994, even TV had a two hour story on ancient prophets. It said much of what Our Lady was warning us all over the world. A prophet had seen a vision of storms, tornadoes and earthquakes. California had dropped into the Pacific Ocean and the East coast was vastly trimmed. Louisiana was flooded by the gulf. Denver and the Rockies were now the West coast of the Pacific. The graphic map of the United States after the storm was a shock.

Another Piece of the Puzzle

The Holy Spirit then gave Father Carroll another piece of the puzzle. To prepare for the return of Jesus Christ through his Divine Mercy, our community needed to do certain things:

1. *Get the people to go to confession on March 15, 1994.*
2. *Prepare to make the Total Consecration to the Sacred Heart through the Immaculate Heart of Mary on March 25, 1994.*
3. *Plan to do the Novena of Divine Mercy from Good Friday to the Sunday after Easter, which is Mercy Sunday. For two years we had celebrated Mercy Sunday. After every daily Mass during the nine day period, the prayer warriors said the Divine Mercy Novena of Sister Faustina.*

How could Father Carroll get them to go to confession, particularly on a week night, March 15? That is where the tickets to the Ark came in.

"This is what you are to say to my children," Our Lady said. "On the fourth Sunday of Lent, called Rejoice Sunday, you are to announce the Good News. Each of you is invited to board the Ark. It is now finished. The time is short. Today is the day of Grace. The Holy Spirit is inviting you to get on the Ark. Bring your children if you want to survive the coming tribulation."

This was the problem. You have to come with your husband or wife, and your children, but you cannot take anything with you but the clothes on your back. You must trust totally in the Sacred Heart of Jesus and his Mercy. You must believe in the scriptures of Genesis; that Mary, the Mother of God, will be used to crush the head of the serpent. You see, the Ark is not only a boat; it is Mary. It is Our Lady who will invite you to board the ship and leave all else behind. This is what total surrender means. As Pope John Paul, II says in his motto "Totus Tuus," you must belong totally to Jesus.

Father Carroll knew what that meant. Many of his children would not sense the coming trials. Some were too busy; after all, everyone wanted a good grade on a test. Everyone had something they were afraid to leave behind. Most were afraid to leave their sins behind.

No Room -- Even for Sin

"I'm sorry," Our Lady told him. "There is no room even for the sins. The only way they can board the ship is give up every little sin."

"On Tuesday, March 15, 1994, the Ark will depart. Only those with a ticket will be allowed to board the Ark; but, the price of a ticket is total surrender," she said.

"How can I teach them?" the old priest inquired. "In fact most of them won't even accept the invitation."

"Don't tell them," Our Lady said, "show them!" "Don't preach surrender; live it and show them how."

Experiencing Divine Mercy

"Many of my priest sons seem never to have experienced Divine Mercy. Therefore, they can't explain it. You, my son, have. Tell them what I did for you. If you do that, I promise many will follow you in the boat Tuesday night. Otherwise, the Remnant will be very small. You have only 6,500 seats plus room for the children. Anyone who doesn't have a ticket will be left behind. And someone else will take their place."

He knew Our Lady meant what she said. On Friday, March 10, 1994, at 2:45 p.m. she told him to order the tickets. "There is no one who loves Jesus enough to rush such an order," he said, "except Dudley. But he doesn't believe in praying to Mary,"

"I will send him a sign," Our Blessed Mother responded.

An hour later Dudley arrived with the tickets and the sign came in the door at the same time. A very devout Lutheran came to get a Rosary blessed.

"For three nights in a row," she said, "a woman appeared to me in a dream and told me to say the Rosary."

"Was she pretty," the secretary asked?

"I couldn't make out her face, it was shaded," responded the Lutheran. "The only thing I could make out clearly was her brown hair that fell over one shoulder. I wanted to put the Rosary around my neck."

"No," the woman in the dream said, "you need to pray it."

"I don't know how," the Lutheran responded.

"Ask a friend," the woman responded, "she will tell you."

The next day a friend gave her a Rosary, a pamphlet that explained the Rosary and told her to get it blessed at St. Margaret Mary Church.

"I am very devout. I pray every day. Now when I wake up, every morning the Rosary is on my mind. I have to learn how to say it."

The Lutheran woman's name is Mary. Father Joe Benson blessed her Rosary. Father Benson told her that Martin Luther had a great devotion to Our Lady even though modern day Lutherans do not. The symbol that Luther borrowed from the Augustinian order can be found today in every Lutheran Church -- it is the Sacred Heart.

The "woman" that the Lutheran saw was the same "woman" whom scripture says in Revelation 12:1, will be "... clothed with the sun, with the moon under her feet, and on her head a crown of twelve stars." It was the Blessed Mother.

"Yes," Our Blessed Mother said, "she will get one of the tickets."

"I hope Dudley and his wife do too," Fr. Carroll said. "They love Jesus so much."

"They got an invitation," Our Lady replied.

Invitation

Our Lady gave the old priest his one chance to convince his children to follow him on the arc. Father Carroll would speak at the 6:00 p.m. and 7:00 p.m. Masses; Father Joe Benson would invite some of the remnant aboard at 8:30 a.m. and 11:30 a.m. Masses. Father Mossy Gallagher will issue the call at the 10:00 a.m. Mass. Father Carroll's sermon began like this:

My Dearest Children,

The Holy Spirit has spent over ten years building up this Remnant Church through Perpetual Adoration, love of Mary and loyalty to the Pope. The Ark is now finished.

You will receive every grace that you will need to survive the coming trials on Tuesday night, March 15th, at 7:00 p.m. at a Penance Service.

When you entered church tonight you received a ticket to board the Ark. You have until after communion to decide if you will accept it. If you choose to reject it, another will go in your place. There is room for only 6,500 plus children. We will leave late Tuesday night. You can bring nothing with you except your children and the clothes on your back. This is what total surrender to Jesus through Mary means.

However, you must be willing to pay the price to trust not me, but Jesus -- totally. Renounce every sin you harbor. Cut through all the lies. On Tuesday night those who accept the invitation will receive an extraordinary grace, the grace to see yourself as you really are. I told you of Father Benson's story (in a recent letter), how when praying this prayer over a group of priests they were literally picked up bodily from their chairs. Father Joe told of the priest who had not gone to confession for 52 years, but went six months before he died. Is it any surprise many of you have soiled your baptismal robes and remained mired in sin? How can I get you to hear this prayer prayed over you on Tuesday night?

Our Lady gave me the answer! Show them!

Friday afternoon Our Blessed Mother gave me the picture. During prayer I saw myself at the Last Supper. I felt the thrill and excitement of the apostles. All but Judas were thrilled as Jesus said the words of consecration over the bread; "...This is my body" and then over the wine, "...This is my Blood ... Do this as a remembrance of me."(Luke 22:19)

I once again felt the ecstasy of my ordination. The words of Latin rang out in my ears; you are a priest according to the order of Melchizedek. The joy of belonging totally to Jesus was indescribable.

My first Mass was reverent and pious. My father, mother, and sister beamed. My brother Ralph, already a priest a year, was there at my side. Tony, my sister's husband looked so young.

Where did it all come apart?

I was then in the Garden of Gethsemane. Tears of blood were streaming down the face of Jesus. Then Christ hit me between the eyes. "I want you to see what your sins have done," Jesus said.

I thought committing sin was just breaking a commandment, but Jesus said, "Sin is breaking our covenant -- it is breaking my heart. It was an agreement you made with God, the Father, through Me, and I must pay dearly for each breach of that love pact."

I knew that once I made the decision to teach you surrender, I would have to pray; "Holy Spirit, let me see myself as I am." Even as I thought of the pain, I winced.

It's no secret to you. I have told you, my children, countless times that I am a sinner. All of a sudden I realized I was responsible, not only for my sins, heavy as they are, but also for your sins.

Just for a moment, imagine me Monday afternoon when I will be kneeling before Father LaFranz, my spiritual director to make a general confession of my life and pray the prayer of total surrender. "Holy Spirit, let me see myself as you see me." I was in the Garden of Gethsemane.

How can I explain to God the Father that I failed to teach you to pray because I was not a man of deep prayer? Then all the sins against the Eucharist will jump up at me. Sure, you will shout, we make sacrilegious communions, but you were our spiritual Father and look at the times you rushed through the Mass.

I knew I would see the face of every child of mine in this community for nearly 25 years who has received communion in mortal sin. There have been thousands of sacrileges.

Jesus will simply ask, "Did you tell them the pain it is costing me?" It's not a broken law. It's a broken body that bleeds for you and me!

How often did I preach Divine Mercy? I can remember the times I heard the confessions of the parish in fifteen minutes. The pain will grow deeper. Sin is breaking a love relationship with God our Father, Jesus our Lord and with our family.

I began to shed tears, real tears, because I realized it wasn't me, Father Carroll in that Garden of Gethsemane; it was Jesus!

Mary told me to tell you the rest of the story. I received Divine Mercy through the outpouring of love in my most sinful moments because Our Lady dragged me, often kicking and screaming, to confession at least once a month. My children, I know from my own experience the healing calm of repentance. I call you to that gift Tuesday night.

The scene moved to the cross. It was Jesus hanging there. I thought he would have criticized or blamed me but he only wanted me to say -- I am sorry.

I looked around and almost everyone had run away. Mary Magdalene, the sinner, Mary the wife of Clopas, John the apostle and Our Blessed Mother were the only four there. What a remnant!

I wanted to take St. John's place and be the priest who would stand by her side. I wanted to comfort Our Lady, but when I looked it was she who was comforting John. Our Lady was comforting all of us, her sinful children -- her priest-sons.

Finally Jesus spoke the words I needed to hear. The words you need to hear. "Father forgive them for they know not what they do."

Tuesday night will be a moment of unheralded grace for this community. This may be your only chance. **It is a moment of Divine Mercy.**

The Holy Spirit has built the Remnant Church - The Ark. Do you have the courage to get in? I'm not asking you to do something I won't do first.

When we gather Tuesday, I will pray this one prayer. "Holy Spirit give each of us the grace to see ourselves as we are." I also will share with you the experience of total surrender to Jesus through the Sacrament of Reconciliation that I will receive on Monday afternoon from Father LaFranz.

Each of you now holds a ticket in your hand. At communion time or before receiving communion ask the Lord if you are truly worthy to receive His Body and Blood in Holy Communion.

If you are in mortal sin, if you have severed your love relationship, your covenant with God, with Jesus, DO NOT, I plead with you, receive Holy Communion unworthily ever again. Instead come up and get a blessing from the priest or lay minister. You will never again be able to plead ignorance before the Father.

St. Paul clearly says, "He who eats and drinks without recognizing the body eats and drinks a judgment on himself." (1 Corinthians 11:29)

Ask for the grace to sign that card, printed by Dudley. Say yes as Mary did. Say yes I will go to confession.

So that's what the tickets were all about. "Yes," the storyteller concluded, "many of us came that Tuesday night. We were all ashamed and scared."

Our Lady was there and many of the children saw angels jumping for joy.

I can still hear the words of Jesus echoing from the cross -- "Father forgive them for they know not what they do."

As I looked around the church that night, to my amazement, there were so few. I later asked the old priest how he felt that night because I saw the tears in his eyes. Most of his children had built the Ark but never rode in it.

"Father, you must have been quite disappointed?" I asked.

"You must have seen my tears," he answered.

I asked the Lord Jesus about it. "Why didn't they listen?"

I heard his answer in a loud tone, "They didn't listen to me either. That's why I wanted you to call it a remnant -- the few."

Then we all saw Jesus in his dying moments turn to His Mother, "Take care of your son -- take care of all Father Carroll's children -- they are part of the Remnant Church, they are family."

Surrender was a small price we paid for the tickets to heaven; if only the others had listened![10]

Chapter Three
Reconciliation

"She (the Church) cannot cross the threshold of the new millennium without encouraging her children to purify themselves, through repentance, of past errors and instances of infidelity, inconsistency, and slowness to act.[11]
(Pope John Paul, II)

Jesus said: "If you bring your gift to the altar and there recall that your brother has anything against you, leave your gift at the altar, go first to be reconciled with your brother, and then come and offer you gift."
(Matthew 5:23-24)

"Forgiveness of sins brings reconciliation not only with God, but also with the Church"[12]
(Catechism of the Catholic Church)

"The whole power of the sacrament of penance consists in restoring us to God's grace and joining us with Him in an intimate friendship. Reconciliation with God is thus the purpose and effect of this sacrament"[13]
(Catechism of the Catholic Church)

✝✝✝✝✝

The Meaning of Reconciliation

In preparing the Remnant Church for the Triumph of Our Lady, we cannot overlook the important element of reconciliation. During the past three years I have come to realize the importance of this gift of reconciliation. During the period of my own "mini judgment," I had a number of interesting conversations in prayer with Our Lady. Our Blessed Mother wanted to show me that many Catholics don't value the sacrament of penance. Even those who avail themselves of the opportunity of God's forgiveness find it doesn't seem to work for them. I asked Our Lady about this.

Our Lady replied: "Many people only want to go to a 'holy priest.'" She showed me what happens when you follow this out logically -- since so few priests seem to measure up to their mythical standard.

Our Lady sent Father Straub, a very holy priest to St. Margaret Mary. The last day of his mission, Father Straub heard confessions from 9:30 a.m. to 3:30 p.m., but only nine people were able to go to confession to him. "What about the other starving thousands?" Our Lady asked. Fortunately, the priests of the parish were hearing a large number while only a select number went to confession to Father Straub.

Another reason confession doesn't seem to work, Our Lady pointed out, is the lack of sincere repentance. Once again Mary gave me an example. During the sermon on the weekend of March 12-13, everyone was asked to choose to repent. I asked everyone to sign a card, "I will come" and "I will go to confession." March 15, 1994, 1200 adults signed that they would go to confession. I then asked them to simply drop these cards in the basket that would be passed around after communion. "Do not put any money in when this basket is passed around," I clearly instructed everyone.

Many chose not to repent by refusing to sign. At every Mass, despite being told not to put money in the second collection but only those cards of intent; we received nickels, dimes, quarters, and few scattered dollars.

"They were asked to repent," Our Lady said, "But many dropped in small change. That's what their confession is like. They are given the opportunity to come and be converted, and they put in petty change."

Repentance Involves Reconciliation

From the very beginning of my experience of Divine Mercy, Our Lady showed me that true repentance demands reconciliation. Jesus told us Himself, "If you bring your gift to the altar and there recall that your brother has anything against you, leave your gift at the altar, go first to be reconciled with your brother, and then come and offer you gift."(Matthew 5:23-24)

I was drawn to reconcile with members of my family: my father, my brother and my sister. Each encounter was painful as I realized the separation I caused because of my shame. This was a gift of Divine Mercy.

Luther -- Reconciliation Among Christians

One of the most moving events that occurred took place early in the morning of March 12, 1994. I woke to hear Our Lady weeping over Martin Luther. Mary was holding him in her arms. I did not get from this image that Luther was not in heaven. Rather, Our Lady was crying for the hurt his shame has caused to the Body of Christ.

"Your sin," Our Lady said, "was no different than my son Luther's. He loved me and the Sacred Heart of Jesus dearly." Shame is clearly one of Satan's most effective tools.

Martin Luther wanted to reform the Catholic Church. When he came to Rome early in the 16th century, he was scandalized by the lack of belief among high ecclesiastics in the real presence of Christ in the Eucharist.

"All reform begins at the foot of the cross," Our Lady said, "not in disagreements which are from the evil one. I have wept for more than 400 years," Mary said, "over my son Luther."

Luther was right that God speaks to all of His children in sacred scripture. He was wrong in not bringing his shame to the feet of Jesus at Calvary.

I realize, from this brief encounter in prayer with Our Lady, that Luther had suffered the same kind of shame over his priesthood as I had. I pray for the day that reconciliation among all Christian churches occurs and we become "one" as Jesus had prayed.

✝✝✝✝✝

How can Divine Mercy Cause our Families to Become Holy?

We know, from the experience of the priests at Medjugorje, the importance of reconciliation. The Franciscans learned that only when people began to forgive one another from the heart did the Holy Spirit become operative at St. James Church in Medjugorje. Father Jozo, a famous priest associated with the apparitions at Medjugorje, shared what he had learned -- in order to pray from the heart, forgiveness and reconciliation are required.

Divine Mercy Could Change Families

Our divine Savior wants fathers to assume spiritual leadership in their own homes. Just as I stood before my entire congregation and asked forgiveness, so, too, each dad needs to bury his own pride. As spiritual healer of the household, he must call his family together and **ask for forgiveness**. Our dad's have a right to bless their children. The should be a nightly occurrence.

In the final analysis, reconciliation is a gift from God the Father Himself. In October 1995, I had life-threatening surgery. The recovery from an "acute aortic dissection" has taken months. Despite the obvious dangers of this surgery, I knew Our Blessed Mother was at my side. This afforded me ample prayer time, which is easy to neglect when you are busy. Our Blessed Mother pointed out to me during this period of great grace that reconciliation is an on-going process.

I would like to share with you two letters Mary asked me to write when I would be able to do so. One was to my older brother Ralph, who is also a priest. He failed one subject in the third grade and my parents decided it would be advantageous if we would both be in the same grade. I needed to tell him that even though I was supposed to be the smart brother and he the dumb one, he was always "my hero."

The other letter was to Fr. Charles, a priest classmate who is dying. Both of these were tough letters to write. However, I knew it was something Our Lady wanted. Perhaps it might help just one priest somewhere to know how much Our Lady loves her priest sons.

✝✝✝✝✝

To my brother Ralph

Dear Ralph,

I wanted to put into writing my feelings that surfaced within a few days after my heart surgery. The most amazing gift I received from Our Lady was a sense of being under her protective care.

For an individual who has run scared since I was a child, this sense of well being and protection was an extraordinary gift. Despite being aware, at least in a rather general way, of the potentially disastrous results of surgery on the aorta, I was now amazed at my calmness. I knew in my heart that Our Lady would shelter me inside her heart. What was there to fear?

After the surgery, I had some serious talks with Our Lady. I am not a visionary or an inner locutionist. However, when Our Lady wants to get my attention, she knows how.

Now I realize that Mary has an extraordinary love for her priest-sons. We are truly her "heart strings" and she is ours.

As we talked about my freedom from fear, even though I might die in surgery, I couldn't help but think of the video Dad did at the request of his granddaughter, Beth. When I heard that tape, I wanted to cry. I thought of all the ways he had put you down as a child, forcing you to fail a grade, using my success in school as a cudgel against a brother I loved.

I remember the pain of my success that was Dad's mantra: "Ralph, why can't you be smart like your brother?"

His push for perfection in others: "If you would have worked harder, you could have gotten a 100 instead of 97." I could never live up to his unrelenting push, "Why can't you be perfect?"

I remember the pain in your voice 50 years later, "Ralph, don't fail again." Yet, through it all you loved him and respected him. Perhaps the video was a small token from a father who could never say, "I am proud of you Ralph."

Mary showed me, "Your dad was right about one thing," she said, "You would never have gone to the seminary if it were not for your brother Ralph. Have you ever told him that he was always your hero?" Mary asked.

Once Our Lady opened my eyes, I realized how right Dad was about me. I was always a fearful person. Walking in my sleep, even on my last night before we left for St. Benedict in 1946, at age 13, was a clear indication. I was a terribly fearful child. But going to St. Ben with my big brother watching over me I could make it. Because, you see, Ralph, you were always my hero. I could always count on you. I never seemed to have many friends, but I had my big brother.

I could never have dealt with the struggles you went through as "the dumb brother." You had guts. Even in Notre Dame Seminary, being told you had to get all "C's" didn't discourage you. Tragically, even in the high points of your life, I was a thorn in your side. I remember Father Karl Schutten's talk at your dinner following your first Mass. "Richard is back" I wanted to say, tell them about my brother...my hero.

I am enclosing the words from the song "Wind Beneath My Wings" by Bette Midler. They say better than I could ever how, Ralph, you have always been my hero.

Perhaps one of the blessings of my illness will be a greater awareness of how much I have valued your love all my life.

I had the good parishes, the good pastors, and the security of one pastorate. You were not so lucky. You had the worst parishes, pastors, and were moved around at the Archbishop's whim. It's no wonder, even to this day, I can say to you what Our Lady wanted me to share. "Tell your brother."

You are "my hero".

✟✟✟✟✟

To Father Charles - One of Mary's Beloved Priest Sons

Dear Charles,

I am sure that Jimmy shared with you my recent heart surgery. Six weeks ago I awoke at 1:00 a.m. with incredible chest and stomach pains. I felt I was having a heart attack or a stroke. My associate, Fr. Joe Benson, got me to the emergency room at 2:00 a.m. I could hardly walk, My blood pressure was 250/130.

After four days my fever broke and I was able to do the stress test which I failed miserably. I had no circulation in my feet. Fortunately, they didn't give me an angiogram, which the heart specialist wanted. I doubt if I would have survived that procedure.

A young heart doctor operated on me on Friday, October 27 1995. He realized that my heart was fine, but the aorta, the main artery leading from the heart, had peeled apart like an onion. I had a 7-hour operation; he would sew it back together. They told me before the surgery that the odds were not good. I later learned that 20% of those having this operation die in surgery; another 20% are permanently paralyzed.

The surgery was a great success. I am now recovering at my rectory. The only damage that is evident is a weak voice. The left vocal cord is paralyzed. Some of this may be corrected by speech therapy which I am taking. I will always have a raspy voice, but that's a small price to pay.

Charles, before and immediately after the surgery, I felt I was under the special protection of Our Lady. I felt like a child hiding inside the heart of my mother.

The surgery has resulted in the healing of some of my relationships, particularly my sister. I also felt Our Blessed Mother has tried to heal some of my relationships with my fellow priests.

Charles, what I would like to say to you is simply this, "I have loved you and all of our priest classmates with a deep abiding love. That love and respect will never be lost. We truly are brothers in the Lord Jesus."

A few days after my surgery, Our Lady tried to help me work through the "perfectionism" that has affected many of us. (I still remember telling my spiritual director at Notre Dame, that I felt perfection was simply an act of the will - decide to love God, and do it.) What arrogance! At least now I can realize that all of us are sinners in need of the saving grace of Jesus Christ.

As I reflected on the group of 52 children, who met for the first time September 1946, I broke down and cried. I felt each of us had failed Our Lady and the Church so badly. The sins of each of us seemed about to overwhelm me.

Then I remembered a picture Diane St. Germain, a parishioner, had painted for my birthday. It had recently been framed and placed in our Evangelization Center. Frankly, I didn't want the picture. Diane didn't want to paint it either. In a dream she was told how she was to paint it. Frankly, I didn't understand it. Our Lady seemed to be rather old and not as beautiful as I imagined Mary to be. In a moment of prayer, just for a moment, it seemed that Our Lady was showing me her heart and how Mary saw you and me, Jimmy and Ralph, Hank and the other children who met in 1946 and were ordained priests.

No, Mary does not see you or me or our brother priests as failures. In an intense moment of ecstasy, it was as if Mary spoke to my heart, "Just love your brother priests, love yourself," she was saying. "Each of you are precious in my sight. No, you aren't failures. You are my precious priest sons."

Charles, I am no visionary or inner locutionist. One thing I am sure of is that Our Lady loves each of us brother priests with unimaginable love and reverence.

I have come to realize that I lack all the great gifts I wished the Holy Spirit would shower upon me. I have only one small gift - the gift of intercession.

I can't get Our Lady to heal people's hearts or illnesses, but Our Lady will never refuse me an intercessory request if I am willing to say yes to her under every circumstance.

I asked for the protection of each of us brother priests of the class of 1946 as well as my own parish. I am sure the answer is yes. The price of this prayer is the heart surgery. I believe many priests are being called to be "intercessors."

Charles, my suspicion is that you too may be a victim soul. I only want you to know how very much I love you. If I am but a small, weak voice, I pray that it resonate inside your heart.

Mary, Our Blessed Mother, loves you as she does each of her priest sons with an unquenchable love. In your moments of trial, Our Lady will shelter you inside her Immaculate Heart.

Love,

Richard

Shortly after he received this letter Fr. Charles called. Another classmate. Fr. Jim, had just died. "I am nearly blind," Fr. Charles said, "I couldn't read your letter, so I asked a friend to read it to me. I will cherish it until the day I die." Fr. Charles died on Wednesday, June 19, 1996.

Chapter Four
Inner Healing

"The primary tasks of the preparation for the Jubilee thus include a renewed appreciation of the presence and activity of the Spirit, who acts within the Church both in the Sacraments, ... and in the variety of charisms, roles and ministries which he inspires for the good of the Church."[14]
(Pope John Paul, II)

"There are sacramental graces, gifts proper to the different sacrament. There are furthermore special graces, also called charisms after the Greek term used by St. Paul and meaning 'favor,' 'gratuitous gift,' 'benefit.' Whatever their character - sometimes it is extraordinary, such as the gift of miracles or of the tongues ... are intended for the common good of the Church. They are at the service of charity which builds up the Church."[15]
(Catechism of the Catholic Church)

✝✝✝✝✝

The Gift of Inner Healing

At a priest's retreat at San Giovanni Rotondo, the monastery in which the late Padre Pio lived, Ms. Kathleen Keefe had gathered a group of priests for a Divine Mercy Retreat, July, 1994. The retreat was entitled "Heal the Shepherd, Heal the Flock." The retreat master was Fr. Bernard J. Bush, S.J. Ph.D. It was an extraordinary opportunity for me personally to begin a process of inner healing.

At this retreat I had the opportunity of meeting Fr. Al Fredette. Fr. Fredette has been a pioneer in prayers for inner healing as well as ancestral healing. He was a great blessing to the priests who attended the retreat in San

Giovanni. He was able to minister to us and was quite generous in sharing the material he has accumulated over the years.

There is a new book entitled *The Power Among us,* the story of a healing ministry. It was complied and edited by Patricia Kelly Ph.D. Dr. Kelly compiled a complete program of inner healing, which has compromised much of the work of Fr. Al Fredette. It has an explanation of inner healing as well as healing of the family tree. It also provides in one location all of the prayers needed by the priest for a "Mass of Inner Healing". It can be purchased from Queenship Publishing Company. Fr. Fredette may be reached by writing to:

>Fr. Fredette
>La Salette
>947 Park Street
>Attleboror, MA. 02703
>Telephone: (508) 222-5410

Fr. Fredette gave the priests at the retreat a copy of the genogram together with a page of the appropriate symbols. There are thousands of possible defects in our own family tree.

Sacred Scripture speaks of the sins of parents being visited on their children down to the third and fourth generation. Fr. Fredette lists some general characteristics to look for.

1. Inherited spiritual defects: from prayerlessness to atheism.
2. Inherited physical defects: such as cancer & heart conditions.
3. Inherited emotional defects: from shyness to tendencies to suicide.

4. Inherited psycho-social defects: from poor spouse communication to unemployment and crime.
5. Inherited social defects: such as divorce, child abuse, etc.

As a religion teacher many years ago I was called by one of my students. She had been bodily thrown out of her house by her father. I picked the young woman up and returned to her home, convincing her father he had acted impulsively. He agreed to take his daughter back.

A week later we were discussing in class, "problem children." "If my kids give me any trouble I will just hit them," the same young woman responded without thinking. Because she had been abused by her father, she was preparing herself to use abuse when she became a mother.

Healing Prayer of Ancestry

Fr. Al Fredette has graciously given his permission to reproduce information on Inner Healing. I would urge Pastors to consider offering a Mass of Inner Healing to help your parishioners deal with shame in their lives.

NOTE: The following three prayers (Healing of Ancestry, Deliverance Prayer, and A Healing Prayer for Family Healings) are recited after communion during the Mass of Inner Healing.

Healing of Ancestry

Eternal Father,
As a community of faith and a family in prayer, we gather to give you praise, adoration and thanksgiving in all things. We pray for all the deceased members of the families represented here, and all those who, in the past, were born deceased still-born, miscarried, aborted, never

committed to God and those who died an early death. We pray for the family members who died brutally or violently, lost in the war or otherwise died from strange and mysterious illnesses, from great fears, acts of cowardice, sudden death, in mysterious fires and for all who were rejected by the family, wanderers and lost members, adopted, abandoned, or rejected.

We pray for all the members of the families represented here who were addicted to drugs, alcohol, games, compulsions of all kinds, gambling, lust, deceitfulness, addictive shopping, and for all family members unduly attached to values of the world, money, prestige, power and control over persons or things.

We pray for those who died and were never prayed for and those buried without a proper funeral. We pray for those who died by their own hand and for those who were murderers or accomplices. We pray for those who died through suffocation or were abandoned, for those afflicted with great phobias, emotional instability; insanity, unexplained illness and from all other causes known by God alone.

We ask release from all bondage coming from the occult, under any form practiced by family members in the past or in the present affecting living members in whatever negative form of bondage, illness, infirmity, emotional or physical illnesses, addictions of any kind, spiritual torment or otherwise confused. I hereby rebuke and cast out in the Name of Jesus Christ, from all living members of these families, the following dark and binding forces of spiritual and emotional torment, undue anxieties, tensions and stress, violence, prejudice, error, devaluation, self-hatred, retaliation, arrogance and deceitful pride in all its forms.

We ask deliverance from fears of all kinds -- the fear of being found out, fear of commitment, fear of failure, the fear of ghosts, the fears of natural elements such as heights, thunder, lightning, wind, water, fire, closed spaces, fearful dreams, the fear of rejection, the fear of man, the fear of woman, the fear of darkness and all other kinds of fears, spiritual, emotional or physical from whatever source.

I hereby rebuke and cast out, in the Name of Jesus Christ all dark and binding forces of superstition, slander, destructive lies and falsehoods, deception in all its forms and attempts to destroy others' reputation, lust, homosexuality, lesbianism, incest and perversions of all kinds, obsessive and compulsive destructive behavior, manic attitudes, depressions, denial and deceitful games, abandonment, excessive anger and rage, guilt, vengeance and self-destructive anxieties, attitudes and attempts.

I hereby rebuke and cast out, in the Name if Jesus Christ, the following dark and binding forces called confusion, chaos, rebellion, arrogance, hallucinations, sleep walking, addictions, fortune telling in all its forms, witchcraft, Satanism, necromancy, santeria, black mass, and occultism in all its forms.

In the Name of Jesus Christ, I rebuke and cast out all deceitful and destructive forces of despair, betrayal, uncontrolled frustrations, bitterness, despondency, repression, projection in all its forms, manipulation and control, the fear of rejection, self-deceit, rejection and self-rejection, exaggerated anxieties, withdrawal, self-pity, false guilt, masturbation and perversions of all kinds. I rebuke and cast out in the Name of Jesus Christ, the dark and binding forces of pride, denial, fantasies, doubt, mockery, repression, hopelessness, fear of insanity, fear of perdition, infidelity, abuse of all kinds, verbal, mental, emotional, physical, or spiritual, false gods and idols.

Seal, I break you in the Name of Jesus Christ.
(repeat the above line three times before continuing)

I hereby break and cast out in the Name of Jesus Christ curses of any kind placed upon the members of the families represented here and all ancestry of these families.

I hereby break and sever by the power of the Word of God and the Sword of the Spirit all negative ancestral spirits and influences of any kind from whatever source, genetic, spiritual, physical, emotional or psychic, affecting the living members of these families wherever they may now be living.

In the name of all these past and lost or injured souls, I ask forgiveness for those who died unforgiven and unforgiving. For them, we ask deliverance from present darkness, confusion and chaos. As a family, we raise up to God all the ancestors who were never baptized for whatever reason. We ask the Lord to accept them, through the baptism of desire, into the family of the Church with a right to Heaven. We bestow upon them all the names of family members who surrounded them at the time of their death. We command the Holy angels to lead all these souls into Paradise to be forever in the Presence of our heavenly Father, the angels, and the saints and from this moment on, to be intercessors for all the living members of the families represented here today. We claim the most Precious Blood of Jesus Christ upon all members of these families, that they be protected from all harm, injury, accident, illness and the wiles of the devil. We also ask the Holy Angels to be, now and always, sentries of protection for all the members of the families represented here today and we ask the angels to protect their possessions from all harm and destructive forces.

We make our prayers in the Name of Jesus of Nazareth whose compassionate love heals all wounds through forgiveness, mercy and prayer. AMEN

NOTE: After the first Healing of Ancestry Mass has been said ... it is important that you attend a Mass in your parish. After the Mass, pray this deliverance prayer so that there will be a continued healing of the living members of your family.

Deliverance Prayer

Dear Heavenly Father,

We praise and glorify you for your love and mercy that you have bestowed upon us and for the spirit of revelation working within us to reveal all hidden sins -- both our own and those from former generations. We now take authority in the name of Jesus Christ over all familial spirits, all generational bondage, all hereditary defects, genetic or of blood, or wrong inclinations that may have been transmitted to us from within our family tree or within spiritual families to which we belong, including the defects within the church that have had their effects upon us personally. By the faith that you give us, we rebuke all sin and the forces of evil that lead to sin. In the holy name of your son, Jesus Christ, we take authority over all familial spirits and bondage, and their manifestations within our lives. By that same power of Jesus, we break the power of evil from ourselves and our families and destroy what otherwise might by transmitted to our descendants. Help us to accomplish your perfect will and fill our hearts and minds with praise of you as we acknowledge your tender mercy. Thank you, Lord, for total healing and deliverance, in Jesus' precious name. AMEN.

A Healing Prayer for Family Healing

Father, I adore you and give you thanks for creating me to be just who I am, my genes, my life conditions, my space in life and time. You created me to enjoy the fullness of life -- your life in me. I believe that you desire to make my family whole and that you have already begun to heal us in all the ways we need healing. Take away my built-in defenses this weekend. Remove all the barriers that prevent healing and my accepting fully your love for me and my family members. I look forward to the time in which your work will be completed and I believe that I will be a channel of that healing for my entire family.

Jesus, I ask for the grace I need to forgive all who have ever hurt me, and I ask to be a representative of my family in receiving grace for all who have hurt any members of my family, individually or collectively. I ask forgiveness from all whom we have hurt. Heal us of all experiences that have made us feel guilty and ashamed; that have caused us to be self-rejecting, and rejecting of one another. Heal me of the rejection real or imagined, of others. Heal me of ridicule and of any incidences in my life or in the life of my family members, that have made us feel unworthy or inferior.

(Take time for the Holy Spirit to bring incidents to your mind.)

Surround me with your light, Jesus, and penetrate the very depths of my being with that light. Let there remain no areas of darkness in me or in my family members, but transform our whole being with the healing light of your love. Open me completely to receive your love, Jesus. Thank you for being our family healer, and my personal healer. AMEN

✝✝✝✝✝

The Eucharist is a powerful means of healing the family tree. We are dealing not just with grace but with the author of grace, Jesus Christ, the Lord himself. Many scriptural passages in the Eucharistic celebration refer directly to the healing power including the ultimate healing "He who feeds on my flesh and drinks my blood has eternal life, and I will raise him up on the last day" (John 6:54.)

I shared the story of Linda Jefferson in *The Remnant Church*. Linda's healing took place in the context of a mass of inner healing. I think it is worthwhile to repeat her story which she shared at all the weekend masses at St. Margaret Mary Jan. 23-24, 1993.

✝✝✝✝✝

Healing of Linda Jefferson

On the weekend of January 23-24, 1993, Linda Jefferson, shared her experience of healing through the Holy Spirit at all the Masses except for the children's Mass. As a young woman, Linda's parents went through a bitter divorce. Angry at God, Linda began to live with her boyfriend and soon became pregnant.

The experience of her first abortion was devastating. As the physician in New York turned the vacuum on, Linda tried to stop him, "It's too late," he told her. As Linda left the doctor's clinic, she vomited on her boyfriend and in his new sports car. The relationship ended and Linda moved to Florida.

Once she relocated, Linda found herself immersed in drugs, alcohol and promiscuous behavior. After a night of drinking, Linda found herself in a stranger's bed. It wasn't

49

long after that she discovered she was pregnant, and an abortion seemed the only logical thing to do. However, complications resulted and she was forced to have a hysterectomy.

It was at this stage in her life that Linda met her husband of twelve years. Despite the grace of sacramental forgiveness in confession and a Catholic marriage, the guilt of abortion remained.

The Holy Spirit led Linda to a contact with a very charismatic priest. He suggested a private mass in which only she and her husband would attend with a priest. During the Mass, she would name her two aborted children, which she did, Cecelia and Gabriel.

During the Mass, an amazing thing occurred. Her husband saw a vision of a woman in white holding two children, a boy and a girl. At that moment Linda screamed out in pain. Our Blessed Mother, took the children back with her to heaven.

Linda herself experienced an amazing healing. Something went through her body from the top of her head to the tip of her toes the moment she cried out in agony. The pain of guilt was completely taken away.

Linda concluded her testimony, sharing one final gift of the Holy Spirit. During a healing service recently at St. Margaret Mary, Linda had a profound religious experience. The Holy Spirit allowed her to see that she had a third child. Her one regret was that due to the hysterectomy, she could never bear a child. Linda was shown by the Holy Spirit that a miscarriage had occurred. This third child would, like her other two children, be in heaven awaiting her arrival.

It took amazing courage for Linda to share her testimony with our community. There was hardly a dry eye in the Church as she told her story. Her life tells not only the enormous gift of mercy that Jesus wants to give us; Linda is a witness to the healing power of the Holy Spirit.

For those who think God will never forgive you for the serious sins you have committed, Linda's testimony was meant for you. In God's eyes, we are all sinners, but we also know that we have Jesus as our Savior.[16]

✟✟✟✟✟

Lisa and Eric - A Powerful Testimony
Monday, April 1, 1996

At the Mass of Inner Healing at St. Margaret Mary on the Monday of Holy Week, Lisa and Eric shared their testimony. Lisa was abused as a child. She and Eric, her husband, were given the gift of "divine illumination" or what is sometimes called the "mini judgment". This is the same grace that I experienced in 1994. Our Blessed Mother at Garabandal (1961-1965) tells us that every human being will go through this experience. Fr. Gobbi in his work *Our Lady Speaks to Her Beloved Priests* mentions the same illumination.

I believe Lisa and Eric's testimony will give you an inkling of what the "mini judgment" will be like. It will help to know that through the gift of Divine Mercy and the Mass of Inner Healing, these problems of the past can be healed.

Lisa and Eric

Lisa: This is a testimony to God's Grace, Mercy and immense Love. Fr. Carroll has been praying for the Grace of each of us to see ourselves as Jesus sees us and this is what we would like to relate to you.

You will remember the two generational healing Masses held several months ago at St. Margaret Mary. Shortly after the second one, as I was praying for the Souls in Purgatory, someone's face came to mind. So, I began praying and realized that this person had died over 25 years ago!

During the next few weeks, I started having flashbacks. At the same time Eric started to grow a beard. I noticed I was upset and repulsed by it - yet I didn't understand why. What I came to realize was that I was a victim of sexual child abuse and the Lord was showing me the connection between the flashbacks and the person's face I had now been praying for.

Eric: On January 20, I awoke at 1:00 a.m. in the morning, Lisa was lying awake next to me. The previous night we had been awakened also in the middle of the night and through God's Mercy, each of us were shown a vision of a table with many things on it. These items were things that we had not dealt with or had not known were hampering our walk with our Lord. Before the night was over, each item on the tables had been presented to us and through His Mercy, removed from our tables.

Now, on this morning I saw a fog roll in and cover the bedroom. I asked Lisa if she could see the fog, she saw a luminous light fill the room. Out of the fog stepped a doctor in green scrubs, a broken baby, a spool of gold thread unrolling and a baby bottle, gold and glowing. The doctor was Jesus and He started sewing the baby together. I was telling Lisa everything as I saw it. She asked if there were any scars on the baby? I said there were none. As Jesus finished, He wrapped the baby in a blanket and started feeding the baby from the baby bottle. It was Lisa being bottle fed of Jesus' love. Then the fog lifted and I was looking into a night sky with lots of stars. I approached a door - opened it and went inside with Jesus. It was like an attic or storeroom. There were broken mirror pieces all over the floor. In walked a young 6 year old Lisa. She was in a party dress with a big, bubbly smile. She walked up to Jesus. He leaned down and picked up 2 pieces of mirror and glued them together. He said, "We'll glue these together and Lisa look!" She looked into the repaired mirror and smiled. No patch marks, the mirror was as new. He said, "Give me a hug," and she did. Then He sent her out to play.

As she left, in walked Lisa - 8 years old. She was in a pretty dress but more solemn and less bouncy. She walked up to Jesus and He leaned down and picked up several pieces of mirror and started gluing them together. When finished, He held it up and said, "Lisa look!" She raised her head and looked into the mirror. She smiled and looked at Jesus. He said, "Go out and play."

As she left, in walked Lisa - 10 years old. She was gloomy and dark. She walked in shyly towards Jesus. He leaned down and gathered up several pieces of mirror and started gluing them together. He said, "I have taken the broken pieces of your self image and I am making it anew to give it back to you whole and new." He held up the mirror, whole and said, "Lisa look!" She said, "I can't!" He said, "Look honey" and she raised her head up and looked into the mirror. She smiled and hugged Jesus. He said, "Go out and play now." She said that she didn't want to. "No you need to go out and play," Jesus said. And she skipped away.

In walked Lisa, 14 years old. She was dressed in
black and very dark. She walked slowly up to
Jesus. He leaned down while saying, "So many
pieces, how are we going to hold it together?" "I
know," he said, "I'll build a frame," Jesus pulled
out small pieces of wood and a little hammer and
nails and built a frame, right there. (I remember
thinking, he is a carpenter, you know). He glued
the mirrored pieces together and inserted it into the
frame and held it up. "Look Lisa!" He said. "I
can't!" she said. At that moment, I heard Lisa's
mom calling, "Lisa!" He said, "Lisa, you must
look!" She slowly raised her eyes and once seeing
herself - her image, she smiled, hugged Jesus and
her mom called again, "Lisa!" "Go and see your
mom," Jesus said. And off she went.

In walked Lisa - 16 years old. She was dragging her
legs behind her and slowly moving towards Jesus.
She was dressed in black and no light was in her,
she was real dark. Jesus looked at the ground and
said, "Look at the pieces, they are just powdered
dust, how can I fix the image? I know, I'll mix the
dust with My love and reform the image." Lisa's
dad called out, "Lisa!" Jesus picked up the dust and
formed a mirror and held it up. "Lisa look!" He
said. "NO", Lisa said. "Lisa, you must look", He
said. "I can't," she said. Lisa's dad called out
again, "Lisa!" Again Jesus asked her to look up and
she looked. At first nothing happened, then Jesus
peeled off some of the black. He remarked, "Three
layers thick." When all the black was off and on
the ground, Lisa smiled and hugged Jesus. He said
for her to go see her dad. Off she went.
Next, Lisa appeared in the corner of the room, she
was 18. She was black and looked like a clump
of clay, not very human looking and hard to
recognized as her. She had a ball and chain on her

foot. Jesus looked at me and said, "There's no more glass. I have nothing to form the image out of. I know, she can look into my eyes and see herself as I see her." "Lisa look!" "NO", she said. "Lisa come her and look" "NO!" again. "Lisa you must try" "NO, I can't."

At this point, the Blessed Mother walked in and across the room to Lisa. She said, "Lisa, give Me you arm - you must get up." "GO AWAY!" Her angel, Anthony tried to pick her up, you must try." "NO, GO AWAY!", Lisa cried.

Mary looked at Jesus and said, "Is there anything in Me that you can use to help her?" With that Jesus walked over to Lisa, bent down and picked her up. They hugged, and the ball fell off her leg. At first, His light didn't penetrate her, then a beam broke forth and out her back - shattering pieces of her and the darkness. Then another one and another one. Then all the black fell off and she stood there in her wedding dress, radiant, hugging Jesus. Then He said, "I have a gift for you." Jesus turned to Eric - I was black. I said, "Jesus, No, look at me." He drew me close and hugged me and I too became white.

He then said, while shouldering a cross -- "I will stand here and hold this cross, heavy with all this broken glass, forever - out of love for you. Now, go forth and multiply My love and bring it to others."

Then He said, "Now pray for your children." One by one I prayed for each one and their concerns. When I was finished, He said, "and mourn the children that you would not conceive." Afterwards, I turned to Lisa and in a dark room, she was illuminated, glowing!! I said, "Lisa you're glowing."

Lisa: To end this testimony, Jesus has, through His great mercy, allowed me to see myself as   He sees me and helps me to address each area of my past that was in need of healing. I have come a long way with His help and I know that He is still calling me to further growth. He has touched the root of many of the problems of my past, and I must now   walk with Him along this new path wherever He leads me.

Eric and I pray that you too, each one of you, will soon be given the opportunity through our Lord's Divine Mercy to see yourselves as He sees you and have the courage to allow Him to heal any part of your lives that needs His Touch.

Chapter Five
Obstacles to Divine Mercy

Obstacle One
The Ministry of Healing - Different than Protestants

As pastor of St. Margaret Mary it is my responsibility to encourage, seek out and affirm all the gifts within our community including the gift of healing. As pastor it is also my responsibility to maintain a clear line of responsibility or authority in the manifestation of these gifts.

In the private sector, it is not the responsibility of the pastor to control the manifestation of the gifts. Thus it would be inappropriate for a pastor to decide that, "no parishioners will speak in tongues in your home." If an individual decides to pray over another in the privacy of his home, this is not the responsibility of the pastor.

In the public sector, in the church or any area of church facilities, the pastor has the clear responsibility to monitor and judge the advisability of exercising any gifts.

Any action or reaction that results from misuse of a gift on church property clearly places the Catholic Church in the position of being subject to legal action. The Church is presumed to be party to any action even though the pastor may not even be aware of what is going on. An example -- a 17 year old in the gym was reported counseling other teens because some adult thought "he has the gift of discernment." This is wrong and was not tolerated.

The Holy Spirit has led this community along a narrow path since adoration began in 1983. I have a very clear sense that the gifts of healing will be important in the coming months. It is also clear that healing will be primarily a manifestation of the Father's desire to bring people to salvation (i.e. intimately connected with evangelization). Scripture speaks of signs and wonders that followed (not preceded) the preaching of the gospel message. Thus I feel the powerful works of healing will be an outgrowth of our evangelization efforts, as well as intercessory prayer.

It is my responsibility as pastor to oversee the public manifestation of the gifts of healing as part of the ministry of St. Margaret Mary. To that end, praying privately over individuals on church property or in the exercise of any ministry which is perceived as part and parcel of St. Margaret Mary is carefully regulated.

Rules for Discernment

A. No one should assume the responsibility of publicly praying over another in church facilities without the specific delegation of the pastor, Fr. Carroll or his delegates, Fr. Gallagher or Fr. Benson.

B. Members of the healing team are specifically recruited. No one will assume the responsibility simply because they attended a workshop.

C. Every member of the St. Margaret Mary prayer healing team is expected to undergo intensive training and be deputed by the pastor or his delegates.

No one should presume to have the right to publicly engage in the healing ministry on church property or as a member of a healing team without the presence of a priest or the specific delegation of the pastor or his delegate on a per occurrence basis. Should a healing team of St. Margaret Mary be deputed to engage in this ministry without a priest, a report will be sent as soon as possible to the pastor or his delegate reporting the results of this intercession.

The Catholic Church vision of the healing ministry is clearly different from our Protestant brothers and sisters. Protestants see the gift of healing quite apart from the organization structure of the church (i.e. a gift given to an individual). On the other hand the Catholic Church sees the gift of healing both within the sacramental system (Mass and Anointing of the Sick) and outside the sacramental system as subject to Church authority. The priest has the gift of Holy Orders and should be part of this ministry.

The Catholic Church specifically condemns the use of the church's full prayer of exorcism without permission of the Bishop. This exorcist must be grounded in the spiritual life and supported in prayer and fasting before an official exorcism can take place, and delegation be given by the Bishop. The danger of the demonic is certainly much greater today than ever before.

Prayer of healing over children or adolescents should be limited to public occasions with a priest participating. A retreat, workshop or healing Mass is an appropriate public occasion for such prayer. This type of prayer should not be used as a feel good therapy, or occasion for seeking spiritual highs.

Finally, it is our belief that the Holy Spirit will bring our entire healing ministry through an intensive period of discernment. If we err it should be in the area of caution.

I am particularly concerned that any priest or laymen should not be involved in St. Margaret Mary healing ministry unless they are willing to be under authority and clearly perceived by the community to possess the quality of humility. Without humility we risk destroying the very fabric of our defense system against Satan. It is too important a risk simply to satisfy anyone's ego, priest or layman.

✟✟✟✟✟

Obstacle Two
Shame

Father James M. Bowler S.J. did a workshop in New Orleans March 9, 1996 entitled "Shame; Friend and Enemy of Spiritual Growth and Wholeness." Fr. Bowler, who works at the Guelph Centre for Spirituality in Guelph, Ontario (phone number: 519-824-125), gracefully granted me permission to quote from the workshop that he did in New Orleans.

Fr. Bowler makes two important points about shame.
1.   The importance of addressing shame issues in order for significant movement to occur in one's journey toward self and God.
2.   Necessity for spiritual directors to confront their own shame issues in order to minister to others.

Fr. Bowler points out that "shame is not guilt." Guilt is: "a disturbing emotion activated when one becomes aware that she-he has behaved in a manner to bring harm to another or to breach some important standard or norm of morality."

"Shame on the other hand refers to the feeling one has about one's very self. This self-alienating emotion tells one that there is some fundamental flaw - however difficult to define - that renders him or her unworthy."

Fr. Bowler goes on to state that shame: "... has the power of inducing feelings of inadequacy toward oneself, inferiority toward others, and deficiency in relationship to God. Unless this state of embarrassment is dealt with, it can effect a formidable hindrance relative to human spiritual growth."

"In contemporary culture, twelve-step programs for all types of dysfunctionality are proliferating ... They also offer relief for the pang of shame defined above as 'the startling realization that we are frail, vulnerable and finite human beings, no different than the vulnerable people we see around us.' However, the desire for healing manifested by participants in any twelve-step program is also the authentic Christian experience of one's need for God. Often it is this need for healing that is not acknowledged or responded to through participation in institutional religion."

Fr. Bowler concludes: "It would be an understatement to say that the majority of people suffer from the reality of shame and will defend themselves from the painful reality at all cost. In his formidable work on shame, Donald Nathanson suggests four major patterns for doing this which he calls the 'compass of shame." These are withdrawal, attacking self, attacking others and avoidance, behavioral patterns with which all those in the ministry of spiritual direction are familiar."

James Bowler claims that "release from a pervasive sense of disgrace shame requires acknowledgment and exposure of the defect or lack to a trusted other or others and the undertaking of substantial change in one's way of being a self." ... true self which is flawed, vulnerable and limited rather than the false idealized self one has employed to navigate the turf of life. A critical juncture in this human spiritual journey is to integrate these two selves and return to the true self all the energy the false idealized self spends defending itself. It is a conversion from narcissistic entitlement to **genuine humility** or from unhealthy to healthy shame."[17]

In my brief conversation with Fr. Bowler, he mentioned that Jesus is shown in scripture healing shame more often than physical healings. Examples of this type of healing are the woman caught in adultery, the Samaritan woman at the well, and St. Peter, who denied that he even knew Jesus. Christ cured their shame.

The Woman Caught in Adultery (John 8)

Perhaps you can better understand this issue of shame if you meditate of the woman caught in adultery. Jesus was in the temple area and began to teach the people who were coming to him. In an effort to trap him the scribes and Pharisees led a woman forward who had been caught in adultery. "They made her stand there in front of everyone. 'Teacher.' they said to him, 'this woman has been caught in the act of adultery. In the law, Moses ordered such women to be stoned. What do you have to say about the case?' (They were posing this question to trap him, so they would have something to accuse him of.) Jesus bent down and started tracing on the ground with his finger."

Imagine the shame of this woman! The Mosaic Law was clear, take her to the walls of Jerusalem and stone her to death. Can you feel her sense of shame? Was she a prostitute? Why did she need the money? Why wasn't the man punished as well? Scripture is silent about these issues.

This is the only time in scripture we are told that Jesus wrote. He wrote in sand. Scholars believe he was writing the sins of her accusers. But they persisted.

"When they persisted in their questioning, he straightened up and said to them, 'let the man among you who has no sin be the first to cast a stone at her.' A second time he bent down and wrote on the ground."

Can you see yourself as one of the accusers? You are angry because Jesus seems to be "breaking the Mosaic Law", but when you look down at what Jesus wrote you see your own sinfulness. What right do you have to stone this woman, when your own sins are worse than hers?

"Then the audience drifted away one by one, beginning with the elders. This left him alone with the woman, who continued to stand there before him. Jesus finally straightened up and said to her, 'Woman where did they all disappear to? Has no one condemned you?' 'No one, sir' she answered."

Here you see Divine Mercy in its simplest form. Jesus was sinless. Would he follow the letter of the law? He had a "right" to stone her. But what does he do?

"'Nor do I condemn you. You may go. But from now on, avoid this sin.'"

Can you imagine the relief that came over that repentant woman. Jesus didn't heal her bodily. He gave her what she needed. He gave her true love - forgiveness of her sins- but even more than that, Jesus cured her of her self hatred. Jesus healed her shame.

We are told by some early Christian writers that this woman was actually Mary Magdelene. She would later go into the home of a rich man, taking some costly perfume and she would wash Jesus' feet with her tears and dry them with her beautiful hair. Jesus had cured her of her shame.

In the same gospel St. John tells us that there were only four people who stood near the cross of Jesus. In John 19:25 we are told that Our Blessed Mother, Mary, the wife of Clopas, and St. John are joined by Mary Madgelene. The woman who had been cured of her shame would share in the shame of the crucifixion.

The Romans knew how to totally shame a criminal. The one to be crucified was stripped naked, nailed to the cross and allowed to die in agony. If we could only understand not merely the suffering but the shame of the crucifixion, we could appreciate what St. Paul meant when he wrote to the Romans:

> "For if you confess with your lips that Jesus is Lord, and believe in your heart that God raised him from the dead, you will be saved. Faith in the heart leads to justification, confession on the lips to salvation. Scripture says, "no one who believes in him will be put to shame." (Romans 9:11)

"Jesus has Carried Your Shame"

In *The Remnant Church*, I shared the feelings I experienced when I learned what was really keeping me from a deep relationship with Jesus Christ. Mary, Our Mother, put it very simply. "When you are ashamed of your priesthood, when you are ashamed of being a priest or of other priests, then you are ashamed of Jesus my Son." But Mary always knows how to reach my heart. She looked directly into my eyes, as only a mother can do and said, "When you are ashamed of being a priest, you are ashamed of me, your mother." I began to cry and couldn't stop crying. How could I ever be ashamed of her. Mary has always been at my side, in my most trying times of my life.

Quickly, Our Lady pointed out to me that Jesus had already carried my shame, just as he carried your shame on Calvary. Mary brought me to the foot of Calvary. There I saw in my mind's eye, Jesus hanging on the cross. I heard him utter the words I needed most to hear, "Father, forgive Richard, for he did not know what he was doing." Incredibly the burden of shame was lifted from my shoulder and my heart.

We were given a picture of Our Lady of Sorrows which now hangs in our Chapel. It was placed there so that our parishioners might imagine what their own "mini-judgment" or "illumination" will be like. As you look at this painting you see Jesus taken down from the cross, laying in the arms of His mother, Mary. When you see yourself as God the Father sees you, you will not be confronted with the long lists of sins you have confessed in the Sacrament of Penance. These have been forgiven years ago.

You are going to realize that what has kept you from a deep relationship with Jesus Christ is your shame. Are you shamed by sin? Are you ashamed of being a Catholic? Are you ashamed of your priests? Are you ashamed of being illegitimate? Only you know what it is that you are ashamed of.

Reconciliation

After my recent life threatening surgery in October, 1995, I felt the presence of Our Lady constantly at my side. Our Lady told me to tell you, "as long as I am at your side, what do you have to fear?" Mary is next to you at this very moment.

As a good mother Our Lady knew that I still didn't fully understand Divine Mercy. Yes, it was important to go to confession. The night before 1200 parishioners went to confession on March 15, 1994 Mary had me make a general confession to my spiritual director, Fr. LaFranz, who recently died. She still drags me to the Sacrament of Penance every two weeks, sometimes screaming and hollering. Yes, repentance is necessary for Divine Mercy to be effective in our lives.

✝✝✝✝✝

A failure to be reconciled is often due to a lack of humility. In view of the fact that our community has been called to intercessory prayer, the virtue of humility takes on added importance.

Our Lady has shown me in countless ways, that you and I will never be an "intercessor" until we learn humility. I believe that was one of the reasons she has gently led me from one trial to another. We can't be an intercessor without humility. Otherwise, whatever gifts the Holy Spirit gives to this community, we will take personal credit for them instead of realizing we are only small instruments in her hands.

Whom do you Need to be Reconciled With?

As I was recovering at Slidell Hospital Our Lady pointed out that Divine Mercy has a third component - reconciliation. She told me I must write to my sister, brother, a classmate who was dying, and a priest that I had inadvertently hurt. As soon as I recovered I wrote a letter to each of these.

For many of you there is probably someone with whom you may need to be reconciled. It may be a deceased or divorced parent, a former friend or spouse, or someone who hurt you as a child.

I asked Fr. Benson, who was adopted, to model this act of reconciliation by writing to his birth mother. When you experience his pain, you will understand a little better why Mary loves priests so very much, why she calls us in Fr. Gobbi's messages "My beloved priest sons." As you read Fr. Bensons letter I want you to imagine in your mind, Our Lady holding him in her arms, just as she is holding Jesus in her arms under the cross. Ask Mary, as you pray, to protect all the priests you have known, all the priests who have embarrassed you or hurt you. Try to experience our pain, our shame. Then you will know why Mary begs you constantly to pray for her priest sons. Then you will understand Divine Mercy.

✠✠✠✠✠

The Rest of the Story

Fr. Benson's letter is to his birth mother. When he talks about his mother in his sermons it is always the mother who adopted him. Now you are going to hear the rest of the story.

When Fr. Joe was 18, he entered the Redemptorist Seminary. But in order to get into the seminary he had to present a Baptismal Certificate. It was at this time he learned he was adopted. He had never met his birth mother.

Joe was accepted into the Redemptorist Seminary, but he was devastated. Two years later he left the seminary, completed his college work, got degrees equivalent to masters in Education and taught in high school until he was 27.

At that age Joe decided he wanted to become a priest in his own diocese in Ireland. He applied and received marvelous recommendations. It was decided that he would study in Rome to become a Diocesan priest. Joe was clearly on the short path to become a Bishop, because most of the Hierarchy are selected from the Roman students.

To his amazement, however, he received a letter from the chancery. It contained only a few words. They may simply have quoted Canon 984 "irregularities by defect." "An irregularity by defect is one which arises from a lack of some quality required for the reception of an order or for its proper exercise. Ordinarily these irregularities do not imply culpability, though in the case of illegitimacy there is culpability on the part of the parents." This meant very simply that until the new code of canon law was promulgated in 1983, a man who was born illegitimate

67

could not be ordained for his own diocese. He could be ordained for a religious order (i.e. Jesuit or Redemptorist), but not for his home diocese, as a diocesan priest.

As a result, the young man who probably would have studied in Rome and become a Bishop in Ireland had the choice of studying for the Archdiocese of New Orleans or becoming a religious order priest. Fortunately that law has been changed. Joe Benson became a priest for the Archdiocese of New Orleans.

There is one woman I would love to meet and that is the birth mother of Joe Benson. There is no priest I admire more. I love Joe like a brother. He is an extraordinarily gifted priest. If I met his birth mother, I would thank her for the gift of life she gave to Joe, and through him the gift of supernatural life that has come to countless others. She could have avoided the shame of being an unwed mother. But she chose life. Thirty-four million children have been aborted in this country alone since 1974; many by Catholic mothers. I wonder how many great priests were never given a chance. All because of "shame" -- a shame that Jesus Christ carried for each of us on Calvary.

I asked Joe to write a letter to his birth mother and thank her for the gift of life, even though he has never met her. Even priests carry the baggage of "shame." As Joe shares his love letter to his mother, I hope his courage gives you the will to never again criticize your priests. Because if you look carefully at the picture of Our Sorrowful Mother that now hangs on our Chapel wall, you will notice it is not Jesus who rests in the arms of Our Lady, it is Fr. Joe Benson, it's Fr. Mossy Gallagher, it's Fr. Carroll. Mary carries in her arms all of her "beloved priest sons."

✝✝✝✝

Fr. Joe Benson's Letter to his Birth Mother

Dear Margaret,

You know it seems strange to me to be writing to you on first name terms. But that is the way things turned out between us, at this stage at least. I have to address you this way at first because we have to get adjusted to each other. Well readjusted might be a better way to put it.

You see, I am your son of 43 years. It seems such a long time before I could manage to make contact with you. Really much has happened and maybe I need to share a few things with you before I get to the heart of the matter.

I did not know that I had parents other than those I had during my growing up. Oh, some things did not seem to fit but my adoptive parents managed to cover things nicely when I asked awkward questions like who were my God-parents and why was I born in Belfast but baptized in a Cathedral 40 miles away from Belfast. I had memories of a large building where I seemed to stay for long periods. They told me for some years that because they both had to work hard they thought it best to put me in this place; and you know, I kind of accepted it, because I didn't want to know anything different.

Well, Margaret, something happened to change all that.

I decided to become a priest !! Yes, dear, a priest. When, at 18, I needed to get a baptismal certificate, Mom went to visit one of our parish priests and he advised her to tell me the truth.

I can still remember that day very well, going to my aunt's place, finding her in the kitchen, peeling potatoes. There was something strange in the air, you might say; an uncomfortable stillness. Aunt Sue called to me and told me that Mom was in the bedroom: had something to tell me.

I thought of "Dad", Margaret. He had had an accident at the dockside two years before. I thought he had died. You can imagine how I walked slowly to the room. There was "mom" sitting on the side of the bed. She was in pain. Rubbing her hands, frantically, frenetically. And her voice was coarse, rough, as if she had been crying.

"I have something to tell you", she brokenly said. I could feel her pain. My gut was now taut, frightened for her. I never liked to see her hurt.

Margaret, dear,

I cannot really say how but I beat her to it. It was not "Dad". It was to me and about me she was trying to address.

I broke the terror: "Are you trying to tell me that I'm adopted?" I asked. Digging a thumb into the back of her hand she nodded, holding back a deep sob.

"You know I kind of began to suspect it, Mom", I said putting my hand on her shoulder by her neck.

"But, I need to know this. Am I illegitimate?"

One of the deepest of covered sobs was to erupt at that moment from this woman. With hands still firmly chaffing each other, she buried her head in her chest and motioned her whole body in one big nod.

I was crushed to numbness within but well trained by this woman without. Sitting down beside her I placed my arms around her and tightened my hold. The child was father of the adult for a few seconds.

"It doesn't matter so much. You are who I know as my mother. So you are my mother. Nothing is going to change that."

"Joseph, please don't tell your Dad that you know," she sighed with a certain anxiety, "I don't think he could take the shame of you knowing he is not your father."

Over the next few days I felt relieved that now something of a jigsaw began to fit together. I had characteristics that, even at 18 were not anywhere in my parents. I was just a little too different from them and their family lines. Now a certain sense was being made of it all.

But Margaret,

A hole opened up in me like you would not believe. An emptiness grew in me. A quest surfaced in me that drained out almost two years of energy in me.
Who then am I?

I had another last name that spoke of roots different from those with which I had come to be connected.

I had a place that was miles away from where I grew and was shaped.

I was a sort of stranger to all who I had known for so long as kin.

I was a bastard child.

AND I HAD TO BE SILENT.

Those two years were spent in Redemptorist Seminary. They were spent silently in my room studying fiercely to cover the pain and the inadequacy I felt about myself. They were spent avoiding any deep sharing for fear I would break my promise to be quiet about it all. Two years of many an hour before the Tabernacle in the quiet of the night, crying for understanding, feeling unacceptable, hoping for acceptance at least from Jesus Christ. Two years of borderline depression masked as reservedness.

And then the wonder of the Lord breaking into my pain, the wonder of understanding that all that had happened brought me to the moment of acceptance of God as God would have me accept him, for the I AM that He is. Not for the things he would do for me. And Jesus as my healer, not in the ways I would have him heal but in the ways he knew I needed to be healed and set free. The sight he gave me beyond my small view to the sight of all to whom he would send me and their need to meet him in his way. To recognize that Mercy is offered only to the broken hearted, the truly little ones; not the Pharisees of righteousness.

No, Mother,
I do not write to you to accuse, to blame, or to crush you. I write to share with you your son's deepest pain, and his deepest love. Because, you see, Mom, I could only also pray for you. You, too must have felt the pain of rejection, the abandonment of the righteous ones. No matter what the scene that would play itself out about you and my natural father: about the lie in feeling deeply rejected and therefore objectionable; I could only also pray for you. The gift of my adoptive mother and father was to pray hard for those who hurt you or offended you. To pray that the truth would come out in all its splendor, someday. To suffer for both sides of the situation. To seek the face of God from the dirty cried out face of His Son on a cross. To reach the point of asking for forgiveness, but then to go on, even in

the pain of feeling abandoned to the point of trusting. To the point of accepting.

Mom, I have prayed for your well-being every day since that day in that bedroom when my other mother shared her pain for me with me. I believe that you, too, have had your pains for me and prayed often "with me" to God. You, too have had your questions about my well-being and purposefulness. My love for Mary has revealed itself as a loving mother too, who has seen her Son raise this little kid up by means of all of you mothers of mine.

Margaret, you are my mother too. I truly and deeply accept you in my heart.. I thank you for my birth. I thank you for being where I have been over these 43 years. I thank you that you are so much a part of me, you might just be proud of this little kid when we meet.

And I hope and I pray, Mom, that if, perchance you might have little to speak well of yourself before the throne of God, you would be surprised and delighted to hear my voice unite with Jesus and say; she gave life to one of the little ones in whom I am to be found.

As much as I want to be there myself, I so much want you to be there, with Dad and my adoptive parents and Mary, Our Blessed Mother. I so much want you to know the joy of my loving you, even from this distance.

Margaret,

You are my mother

I am your Son.

I love you.

Your Son, Joseph

While Father Benson was reading his letter to his birth mother, Margaret, tears were flowing like a river. It was a remarkable testimony. As Joe shared the shame he had endured, each person could recognize that the priesthood is a sharing in the sufferings of Jesus Christ. As soon as the priest finished, there was spontaneous, standing ovation for his courage and humility.

✝✝✝✝✝

Conclusion

Prior to the onset of the chastisement, God in His mercy will offer the church a brief opportunity to touch the hearts and minds of the world's people. We must be ready for it. As St. Paul says, "we beg you not to receive the grace of God in vain ... now is the acceptable time. Now is the day of salvation."

What does the Catholic Church need in her pastors in these times called by Pope John Paul, II the end times? Do we need pastors who tell us what a wonderful job we are doing and send us off each week with a false sense of security ... feeling good about ourselves? Or do we need pastors willing to recognize the signs of the time, to tell his flock what Our Lady has said in every part of the world, "My children are not prepared"? We need priests willing to be watchmen; to stand at the gates and sound the trumpet of warning. God the Father will forgive his priests if they sound a warning which turns out to be premature; but God help those pastors who fail to warn their flocks. The flocks will be scattered and Satan will wreak havoc. And God will hold the shepherds responsible.

The warning is very clear. I believe Fr. Gobbi's time table. It will all be over by the turn of the century. You who have been prepared will live through the greatest era of

peace the world has ever seen. The Era of Peace promised
by Our Lady at Fatima in 1917, is soon to be realized.

[1] Sister M. Faustina Kowalska, *Divine Mercy in My Soul: Diary*,
(Stockbridge, Massachusetts: Marian Press, 1987), #1520.

[2] *Catechism of the Catholic Church*, (New York: Catholic Book
Publishing Co., 1992), pages 634, #2635.

[3] Carroll, Richard, *The Remnant Church*, (Chelsea, Michigan: Book
Crafters, 1993), pages 177-180.

[4] Pope John Paul, II, *Tertio Millennio Adveniente*, (Boston, MA.:
Pauline Books & Media, 1994), page 37, #32.

[5] (*Catechism of the Catholic Church*, page 257, #986.)

[6] The Total Consecration includes a thirty-three day preparation
outlined by St. Louis de Montforte. We become slaves to
Jesus through Mary. Pope John Paul, II makes this
consecration daily.

[7] Alphonse Cappa, S.S.P., *Fatima Cove of Wonders* (Boston, Ma.:
Daughters of St. Paul).

[8] Pope John Paul, II *On the Mercy of God*,

[9] (Carroll, *The Remnant Church*, Pages 186-191.)

[10] (Ibid, Pages 191-204.)

[11] (Pope John Paul, II, *Tertio Millennio Adveniente*, page 38, #33.)

[12] (*Catechism of the Catholic Church*, page 367, #1462.)

[13] (Ibid, page 369, #1468.)

[14] (Pope John Paul, II, *Tertio Millennio Adveniente*, page 50, #45.)

[15] (*Catechism of the Catholic Church*, page 485, #2003.)

[16] (Carroll, *The Remnant Church*, Pages 164-166.)

[17] Bowler, Fr. James, From a workshop entitled "Shame, Friend &
Enemy of Spiritual Growth and Wholeness" held at the Jesuit
Center on the Loyola University Campus in New Orleans,
La. on March 9, 1996.

JESUS IS LORD

Section Two
Discipleship
Year One -- Jesus is Lord -- 1997

"The first year, 1997, will thus be devoted to reflection on Christ, the Word of God, made man by the power of the Holy Spirit."[1]
(Pope John Paul, II)

"Incorporated into Christ by Baptism, Christians are 'dead to sin and alive to God in Christ Jesus' and so participate in the life of the risen Lord. Following Christ and united with him Christians can strive to be 'imitators of God as beloved children, and walk in love' by conforming their thoughts, words and actions to the 'mind .. which is yours in Christ Jesus', and by following his example"[2]
(Catechism of the Catholic Church)

Chapter One
Discipleship a Form of Evangelization

"The whole Church is preparing for the third Christian millennium. The challenge of the Great Jubilee of the year 2000 is the new evangelization: a deepening of faith and a vigorous response to the Christian vocation to holiness and service"[3]
(Pope John Paul, II)

✠ ✠ ✠ ✠

Discipleship

On the weekend of June 22-24, 1996 I participated in a unity conference at the Ramada Inn near the International Airport in Philadelphia, Pa. The title of my talk was "A Parish United."

The purpose of this conference at Rosemont, Pa. was to bring together charismatic, marianists, marriage encounter, Cursillo and other spirit filled groups in the Catholic Church.

Prior to my departure a prayerful parishioner, the same woman who warned me that I would endure physical trials a week before I had my life threatening surgery, came in to see me. "Our Lady wants you to know that you will plant seeds at your conference," she said. "However, Mary warns you not to be discouraged if the message seems to go over the heads of the participants."

As I headed for the conference, aware of the limitations of my voice, I felt extremely discouraged. I felt Our Lady was sending me to speak about discipleship to a group who would not be open to what I had to say. All of this for the purpose of "planting seeds."

When I arrived at the Philadelphia Airport I was picked up by a young man by the name of Shawn Ryan and his friend John. Shawn told me an amazing story. John had asked Shawn and Lynn (a friend) to go to the drug store a few weeks earlier to get him some medicine. On the way to the store, Shawn was crossing Franform Avenue at Knorr Street with a green light. A drunk driver ran a red light and plowcd into Shawn's brand new car, hitting the center of the drivers side.

Shawn said, "I remember sitting on the curb looking at my brand new, six week old car. I heard my spirit say, 'Hail Holy Queen, Mother of God!' Then I heard an audible voice speak to me: 'Shawn, my work for you is not yet complete. I want you to go to the "Upper Room" and tell them the fruits of their labors are many. And **most of the seeds sown, are rooted in good soil.**'"

The "Upper Room" is the prayer group of the IHS Network that put on the Unity Conference. This seemed to confirm to me the purpose of my involvement in the Unity Conference -- "to plant seeds."

Shawn continued: "At that time, a vision was revealed to me of a handful of workers in a field. They were sowing seeds, some of which landed in thorny bushes, some on broken rocks and some on soil so rich that the seeds manifested into unending stretches of golden wheat!"

Miraculously both Shawn and Lynn did not have a scratch on either of them. As Shawn looked at the crumpled steel and shattered glass, he realized that the voice and the vision "were of the Blessed Mother." Shawn looked down to see the leather jacket that he had been wearing. It was under the back left wheel of his car.

At the Unity Conference, one participant told of being asked at a business meeting, "who are you?" "I am a disciple of Jesus Christ, cleverly disguised as a systems programmer," she replied.

What does it mean to be a "disciple of Jesus Christ?"

1. It means primarily to have a **personal relationship** with Jesus Christ. It is a relationship of love. Jesus tells us, "whoever loves Father or Mother, son or daughter, more than me is not worthy of me." (Mt 10:37).

As Catholics we come into this relationship through Baptism. This love relationship is nourished by the Eucharist. Jesus said: "if you do not eat the flesh of the Son of Man and drink his blood, you have no life in you." (Jn 6:53). There is simply no closer relationship anyone can have with Jesus Christ than to receive him in the Eucharist. As Catholics we believe that it is Jesus we receive in Holy Communion.

2. Being a disciple of Jesus Christ means **taking up our cross**. "Jesus said to all: 'Whoever wishes to be my follower must deny his very self, take up his cross each day, and follow in my steps."(Luke 9:23) St. Paul put it simply when he said he had come "...to preach Christ crucified."(1 Corinthians 1:23) Sufferings and sacrifice are integral to our relationship to the Lord.

3. Being a disciple of Jesus Christ means **sharing that faith** with others. There are 80 million Americans who are unchurched. The Catholic Church is the largest religious denomination in the USA. Fallen away Catholics are the second largest number.

Jesus said. "Go, therefore, and make disciples of all nations." (Mt. 28:19)

4. Being a disciple of Jesus Christ means **witnessing without fear**. Scripture tells us, "Love has no room for fear; rather, perfect love casts out all fear." (1 John 4:18).

5. Being a disciple of Jesus Christ means **loving his mother**. When Jesus was dying on the cross, he committed each of us to Mary. St. John tells us in his gospel: "Seeing his mother there with the disciple whom he loved, Jesus said to his mother, 'Woman, there is your son.' In turn he said to the disciple, 'There is your mother.' From that hour onward, the disciple took her into his care."(John 19:26-27) If you do not have a relationship with Our Lady, pray every night: "Jesus, teach me to love your mother."

The Vision of the Wheat Field

"The harvest is rich but the workers are few," Jesus said (Luke 10:2). There is soon going to be a tremendous harvest of souls due to the Divine Mercy of Jesus Christ. This harvest will come about through the labors of the disciples of Jesus and through the power of the Holy Spirit.

Once a community can understand Shawn's vision, they will begin to put their priorities in order. Once Jesus Christ becomes Lord of your life, you want to share that love with the millions who have never heard of Jesus. You will want to bring back to the church the millions of Catholics who have left, not simply an institution, but their personal relationship with Jesus Christ.

In 1997 the focus of the Catholic Church will be on Jesus Christ. As we prepare for the third millennium, each of us must commit ourselves to become not passive members of the church, but active, fully armed disciples of Jesus Christ.

Bishop Anthony Pilla put it well: "the Whole Church has been asked by Pope John Paul, II to bring together 'two elements essential to the mission of the church, holiness and evangelization,' ... linking holiness and evangelization leads to the discovery of the new evangelization's essence: 'to become mature ecclesial communities living the Gospel so fully that evangelization flows from the depths of who we are in Christ Jesus.'"[4]

✝✝✝✝✝

A New Form of Evangelization

Bishop Anthony Pilla in addressing 100 Bishops on evangelization reminded them that, "We cannot give what we do not have." The Lord Jesus had led our community at St. Margaret Mary to an awareness that we must truly become "Fully Armed Disciples of Jesus Christ" if we are to evangelize.

A key component of this vision to evangelize was the building of a facility for adult education. However, before the Evangelization Center was complete in May 1995, it was totally flooded. We were finally able to open in September of that year.

The Evangelization Center is a training center. It includes an assembly hall which seats three hundred. We have a classroom which is capable of interactive communications by use of microwave television. We could be a sending as well as a receiving station.

The Evangelization Center has two smaller meeting rooms, a Religious Education office, an adult library and video library, and a large dining room with kitchen equipment. It is clearly an adult building, including adequate restroom facilities. However, it connects to the entire school by covered walks.

With the recent addition of a small satellite dish, we can transmit from the church which seats eight-hundred to the gym (500), the Evangelization Center (total 450), or any of the twenty-seven classrooms. All of these buildings have computers and TV-VCR monitors. In other words, on any given night we could have 2500 individuals involved in one event.

Becoming a Disciple of Jesus Christ

The goal of evangelization at St. Margaret Mary is not simply adult religious education. Our discipleship training program involves study, prayer, retreats, evangelization training, RCIA., and time for adoration of the Blessed Sacrament. Each participant must agree to at least one hour before the Blessed Sacrament each week. Knowledge without prayer is of little value to the Lord.

We ask each participant to commit to a minimum of four years. In order to become a "fully armed disciple of Jesus Christ" each person should try to recruit one disciple a year for four years. They may recruit active Catholics, fallen away Catholics, Protestants or unchurched individuals.

In five years time our goal is 5,000 committed disciples:

1st year (Sept. 1995) = we registered 300 disciples
2nd year (Sept. 1996) = 600 disciples
3rd year (Sept.1997) = 1200 disciples
4th year (Sept. 1998) = 2400 disciples
5th year (Sept. 1999) = 5000 disciples

Incidentally, our second semester we grew from 300 to 430 participants. We are looking forward to our 600 committed adults for the fall 1996 term.

Requirements for Completion

In order to impress upon our parishioners the need for holiness as well as knowledge we outlined a course of studies required to become a fully armed disciple of Jesus Christ. The typical course runs 10 weeks in the fall and 10 weeks in the spring for two hours per week. Each participant is expected to complete the following during a period of four years:

2 years of Scripture
1 year of Theology
    (including either Dogma, Evangelization
    Training, RCIA or Church History).
1 year of Spiritual Direction or Family Ministry.

Father Dwayne Stenzel

We were very fortunate in meeting Father Dwayne Stenzel O.F.M., who is currently the director of a retreat center in Thibodeaux, Louisiana. Father Stenzel conducted an evangelization training school for eight years in Detroit, Michigan, in a seminary facility. Father Stenzel also spent a number of years preaching with an evangelical couple throughout the country. We have received a great deal of help from him in setting up our school of evangelization.

It has been our experience during the first year in operation, that some video tapes can be effective tools where qualified teachers are not available. We were able, in our first year, to have Father Richard Maughan teach a course on Church History. Father Benson with the help of Bonnie Chase taught two courses on the Spiritual Exercises of St. Ignatius. Yvonne Galatas who has a M.A. and serves as the Director of Religious Education directed a course in scripture as did Joe Lajaunie and Richard and June Calkins. Fr. Stan Klores, spiritual director at Notre Dame Seminary in New Orleans, La. taught a course on spirituality in the second semester.

I began in September with Deacon Clarence Vicroy, Deacon John Weber, and Deacon Bob Binney directing the RCIA training. Since 1984, we have an average of over twenty adult converts a year. Serious health problems forced me to give up this position in October, I expect to join my staff of volunteer deacons and qualified RCIA discussion leaders in September, 1996.

The Scott Hahn video tapes were one of the most successful courses taught this year. Deacon Dan Haggerty and Mrs. Veralyn Alpha were the discussion leaders. They both felt these videos were excellent teaching tools.

Mr. and Mrs. Bill St. Cyr were the discussion leaders using Dr. James Dobson's video tapes. They also felt this program was well received.

In the evangelization training program directed by Mike and Doris Osborn, Bill Bright's videos on "Witnessing Without Fear" were quite effective. However, they also had Father Stenzel's outline which proved helpful. The Osborn's have been involved for years in different evangelization training programs. They helped form this group into greeters for both Christmas and Easter Masses.

They also had these individuals calling on newcomers to welcome them to our parish.

The course selection will change and improve each year. Father Joe Benson and Father Mossy Gallagher have helped considerably this year. Father Benson conducted a workshop on healing with Sister Veronica Miceli, a recognized leader in this field, in December 1995. Father Benson has taken over our Youth Retreats with considerable success. Father Mossy Gallagher taught a semester on prayer before the Blessed Sacrament that proved a blessing to many.

The Charismatic Community and the Magnificat Women's Group at St. Margaret Mary have conducted successful Life in the Spirit Retreats. Father Stenzel also held a similar retreat this year at our Evangelization Center.

A Final Note

We have charged a nominal fee for each course except RCIA and Evangelization Training. The $20.00 fee a semester has allowed us to give a reasonable stipend to the "outside experts" who have to travel at night from New Orleans often at a great inconvenience. This small fee has proved a great blessing. If disciples are willing to invest money as well as time, you can be sure people will not miss class unless it is absolutely necessary. A collection is taken up each week at Friday Night Intercessory Prayer during the Mass for our evangelization program.

Schools of Evangelization

I feel that if Father Mossy Gallagher, Father Joe Benson, and I can run a school of evangelization, anyone can. When Dioceses are closing parochial school facilities, it would be helpful to establish regional centers of evangelization. Furnish the building so that adults will feel comfortable, charge a reasonable fee, and pay your professional teachers an adequate stipend. Commitment, prayer, study, and recruitment of disciples comprise the formula for successful evangelization.

For the convenience of any priest wishing to start a school of evangelization, I am reproducing the initial material that we gave out on Monday, September 25, 1995. In the second year we have already modified and, I believe, improved the program.

✞✞✞✞✞

St. Margaret Mary School of Evangelization
Initial Gathering
Monday, September 25, 1995

A Vision for Evangelization

Introduction:
His Excellency Archbishop Schulte in the mission statement of the Archdiocese of New Orleans gives us the key elements needed to evangelize each parish. "We are called to carry the Good News of Jesus Christ from that holy gathering (the Eucharist) to all people of every race, language and way of life." To do this we must become disciples. As the mission statement of the Archdiocese charges us: "We recommit ourselves to growth in the life of faith, to follow with new fervor 'Our Savior's way of holiness,' and to carry on His work by inviting others to "'Taste and see how good the Lord is.'" (Psalm 34:9)

What is Evangelization?

Jesus said "Go into the whole world and proclaim the good news..." (Mark 16:15). Evangelization is the sharing of the Good News for which Jesus Christ was born, suffered, died, and rose. He is Our Savior. Evangelization is the call to proclaim that Jesus Christ is Lord and Savior of our lives.

Jesus is the source of our happiness. He is the treasure we want to share with others. In a recent news program, the question of happiness was studied in detail. It was concluded that money, pleasure or power does not bring happiness. At best, it is a limited commodity.

The Baltimore Catechism studied by most older Catholics gave us the answer to the question, "Where is happiness found?" We were taught that our purpose in life was God. "God made me to know Him, to love Him, to serve Him, and to be happy with Him in heaven." St. Augustine puts it, "Our hearts are restless O God until they will rest in thee."

Changing Culture

We live in a different type of world today. Eighty million Americans are unchurched. Less than fifty percent, perhaps as low as one out of four American Catholics, go to church on Sunday. According to Dr. Barna, a social scientist, the major reason the unchurched give for not attending is, "I don't get anything out of religion." Dr. Barna tells us, however, that they are searching for meaning in their lives as well as meaningful relationships.

As Pastor of St. Margaret Mary, one of my concern is for the salvation of the thousands of parishioners who do not attend church on Sunday. Sadly, many nominal Catholics report that they have never experienced the presence of God. We are encouraged by the words of St. James in his epistle 5:20, "Remember this: the person who brings a sinner back from his way will save his soul from death and cancel a multitude of sins."

A great percentage of Catholics in this country has fallen away from the Catholic faith. Clearly, there is a need to evangelize. We will use *Witnessing Without Fear,* the program by one of the most successful Protestant evangelists in the world, Bill Bright, Director of Campus Crusade for our evangelization class. He conducts evangelization in more than 150 countries.

Campus Crusade challenges many of our young college students with the phrase, "Are you saved?" Having never heard this terminology before, the young Catholics sadly admit, they don't know if they are saved. Many Catholics fall away simply because they don't think that they are "saved" in the Catholic Church.

In our Evangelization Program participants are trained to be **fully armed disciples of Jesus Christ.** You will be able to answer questions such as "Are you saved?" Bill Bright's question comes from St. John 3:5, "... no one can enter into God's kingdom without being begotten of water and Spirit."

It is important to realize that the Greek adverb "anothen" means both "from above" and "again." Jesus means "from above" but Nicodemus misunderstood it as "again." The primary meaning of this text is clearly baptism (i.e., "Born from above.") Hence, salvation comes to us initially from the sacrament of Baptism.

However, in an applied sense this text can mean a personal decision to follow Christ. However, this would be a secondary meaning. The Catholic Church teaches that baptism is absolutely necessary for salvation.

Can Catholics Accept Jesus as Lord and Savior?

The answer to this question is certainly; we can and do accept Jesus as Lord and Savior. Remember, however, scripture teaches that we cannot call Jesus, Lord "... except in the Holy Spirit."(1 Cor. 12:3) Jesus calls us to repent.

There is nothing in the text used by Bill Bright that we as Catholics find objectionable. Can we too make a personal decision to accept Jesus as our Lord and Savior? Absolutely! Protestants call this a "born again experience." Catholics can also have this same experience. We believe there is more to discipleship than inviting Jesus into our lives. To be a complete disciple we must know Jesus through the oral and written traditions of the church. We must find Christ in his sacraments, particularly baptism which is the entry way into grace and the Eucharist which is the reception of the body and blood of Christ. In brief, we must become "fully armed disciples of Jesus Christ." The seven sacraments are the primary ways that we meet Jesus Christ.

Becoming a Fully Armed Disciple of Jesus Christ

In addition to knowing and accepting Jesus as Lord and Savior, we must come to know Christ in His church. It is not only in the word (Scripture) that we can find Jesus, but we can also find Him in the sacraments, particularly the Eucharist.

We experience the presence of Christ in the teachings of Jesus found in the oral and written tradition. It is the Church itself that gives us the Bible. It is the Church that preserves the sacraments and oral teachings of Jesus.

The Bible itself attests to the oral traditions of the Church. St. John ends his Gospel in Chapter 20:30-31 with these words, "Jesus performed many other signs as well --

signs not recorded here -- in the presence of his disciples. But these have been recorded to help you believe that Jesus is the Messiah, the Son of God, so that through this faith you may have life in his name."

A Four Year Program

This program of discipleship called "A Fully Armed Disciple of Jesus Christ," will be a four year program. A Catholic who goes through the four years of training in evangelization will experience Christ through a personal decision to accept Him as Lord and Savior. We will also experience the intimacy of Jesus in oral and written traditions of the Church, especially Baptism and the Holy Eucharist.

There is no greater intimacy than our reception of the Body and Blood of Christ in Holy Communion. We accept John 6:54 as literal, when Jesus tells us, "He who feeds on my flesh and drinks my blood has life eternal ..." Protestants take this as figurative language. If it was not meant to be literal, why didn't Jesus stop His disciples from leaving Him, when most of them said, "This saying is hard; who can accept it?". They refused to believe.

When asked by others, "Are you saved?", what are you to reply? I would be reluctant to say, "Yes, I am saved," for the Bible teaches, "... let anyone who thinks he is standing upright watch out lest he fall!"(1 Cor. 10:12) Those who complete the four year course on evangelization will be able to respond as follows: Through the power and grace of the Holy Spirit, I accept Jesus Christ as Lord, which you call a "born again experience."

I know Jesus, and I have a personal relationship not only through faith in His word (Scriptures). I know Him in an intimate way through the oral and written traditions of the Church, which gave us the Bible itself. I have a love relationship with the Lord in the Sacrament of the Eucharist. I know Jesus through the doctrinal decrees of the Church, especially the Apostles Creed, The Nicene Creed, and the teachings of the Catholic Church founded by Jesus Christ. I know Jesus through my relationship with His Mother, Mary, whom the Church has honored since the Council of Ephesus in 430 as the "Mother of God." Through God's grace and His Divine Mercy, I can say ... I am saved!

My vision for St. Margaret Mary is that we train thousands of fully armed disciples of Jesus Christ through intercessory prayer, study, and spiritual direction. These disciples must have a solid foundation in prayer through Spiritual Direction and Perpetual Adoration and be fully alive with the Holy Spirit through a Life in the Spirit retreat or seminar. Once trained, these disciples will share their faith and love experience with others. The Good News of Jesus Christ will spread throughout Slidell and the New Orleans area.

Pope John Paul II in his apostolic letter, "Tertio Millennio Adveniente," says,
> "While I invite the faithful to raise to the Lord fervent prayers to obtain the light and assistance necessary for the preparation and celebration of the forthcoming jubilee (i.e. Year 2000), I exhort my Venerable Brothers in the Episcopate and the ecclesial communities entrusted to them to open their hearts to the promptings of the Spirit. He will not fail to arouse enthusiasm and lead people to celebrate the Jubilee with renewed faith and generous participation"[5]

We have distributed hundreds of Holy pictures of Divine Mercy to Catholics and non-Catholics alike. These holy pictures commemorated my twenty-five years as Pastor of St. Margaret Mary, January 17, 1995. On the back is a prayer adapted by Father Stenzel O.F.M. utilizing the simple prayer of Bill Bright..... Jesus is Lord! This prayer summarizes my vision of the Remnant Church..... We are a group of people who know that each of us is a sinner. We also know that Jesus is our Lord and Savior. Each one of us can say what the late Bishop Sheen wrote, "I thank God I am a sinner, now I can have Jesus Christ as My Savior."

"Lord God, I confess that I am a sinner. I confess that I need Your Son Jesus. Please forgive me in His Name. Lord Jesus, I believe You died for me and that You are alive and listening to me now. I now turn from my sins and welcome You into my Heart. Come and take control of my life. Make me the kind of person You want me to be. Thank You for loving me, for forgiving me and for coming to live in my heart -- never to leave or forsake me. Now, fill me with Your Holy Spirit, who will show me how to live for You and acknowledge You before men as my Savior and my Lord. I love you Jesus. Amen"

✞✞✞✞✞

Evangelization 2000

St. Margaret Mary mails out at least twice a year a newspaper which was entitled "Evangelization 2000," but is now called "Go Into the Fields." This newsletter contained personal testimonies, which are the **most effective form of evangelization**. We send this to every individual household in our parish boundaries churched and unchurched.

Just as Pope John Paul II pointed out in his encyclical on the coming of the Third Millennium, Mary points to her Divine Son and she is proposed to all believers as the model of faith which is put into practice. Each of us in the remnant church goes like a child to its mother and asks Our Blessed Mother to "teach us how to pray." Once we learn to surrender to Jesus through Mary, the Holy Spirit will teach us how to make Jesus the Lord of our lives. Then we will become fully armed disciples of Jesus Christ and willing to share our own faith experience with others.

As Our Holy Father put it so well linking evangelization and holiness and offering them as the "essential elements of jubilee observance."

Chapter Two
The Bible

"In order to recognize who Christ truly is, Christians, especially in the course of this year, should turn with renewed interest to the Bible, 'whether it be through the liturgy, rich in the divine word, or through devotional reading, or through instructions suitable for the purpose and other aids.' In the revealed text it is the Heavenly Father himself who comes to us in love and who dwells with us, disclosing to us the nature of his only-begotten Son and his plan of salvation for humanity."[6]
(Pope John Paul, II)

"This emphasis on the centrality of Christ, of the word of God and of faith ought to inspire interest among Christians of other denominations and meet with a favorable response from them."[7]
(Pope John Paul, II)

The Holy Father encourages us to use the Bible as a means of knowing Jesus Christ. We know Jesus through His own words, as well as listening to Him speaking to our hearts. There are two basic ways to approach Sacred Scriptures.

1.   What does this text in Scripture mean to me in my life. *A Pilgrim's Way* uses this approach to bible study.

2.   What is the meaning of the text (exegesis) of Sacred Scripture intended by it's authors. This scholarly approach to the Bible is utilized by the Denver Catholic Biblical School Program.

A Pilgrim's Way Bible Study

"We are a pilgrim people. We have been called to a journey through this life, sustained by faith, toward our heavenly goal. We have been called to pray with and for one another, and to strengthen one another through the witness of our personal holiness.

"*A Pilgrim's Way* enriches this pilgrim experience through a guided searching of the Scriptures, together with an interaction of prayerful study and reflection with others. From this sharing of Scripture, there emerges an awareness that, while we are pilgrims, we are not solitary pilgrims. There comes a deepened sense of community. There comes a personal bonding with others. There is a unique blend of information (growth in knowledge), formation (experience of an ecclesial community), a spirit of prayer (a new hunger for greater intimacy with the Lord), and a readiness for further progress in one's committed life as a Christian."[8] Competent laymen can be utilized as discussion leaders in the Pilgrim's Way Bible study.

The Denver Catholic Biblical School Program

THE DENVER CATHOLIC BIBLICAL SCHOOL PROGRAM is one of the most successful Catholic Bible training programs ever developed. "Over 800 people in the Denver area are enrolled in or have completed the ... course that covers all aspects of Bible study and examines every book of the Bible. It is nationally acclaimed as the best training program for preparing leaders in Bible study for parishes and home study groups."

Year One: OLD TESTAMENT FOUNDATIONS: *GENESIS* through *KINGS*. "The First Year Program covers the first two major sections of the Old Testament: the Pentateuch and the historical books that make up the Deuteronomic History of Israel. It is a full introduction to the foundational books of the Old Testament and their most important historical, interpretive and theological questions.

"Year Two: NEW TESTAMENT FOUNDATIONS: JESUS AND DISCIPLESHIP introduces us to the writings of the New Testament. It begins with an examination of what makes up a gospel and the unique viewpoint of each evangelist. It then examines the nature of St. Paul's letters and their profound theology of the risen Christ, and concludes with the study of the special literary and theological approach of John's gospel and the book of Revelation. All materials from each type of writing allow us to learn more fully about the early Christian communities that produced them." [9]

Father Frank Montalbano OMI, a scripture scholar and instructor at Notre Dame Seminary in New Orleans, LA. will direct this program, beginning September, 1996.

Chapter Three
Obstacles to Discipleship

Obstacle One
Satan

"We (the Church) put on the armor of God that we may be able to stand against the wiles of the devil and resist on the evil day (cf. Eph. 6:11-13)."[10]

"Man, tempted by the devil, let his trust in his Creator die in his heart and, abusing his freedom, disobeyed God's command. This is what man's first sin consisted of. All subsequent sin would be disobedience toward God and lack of trust in His goodness"[11]
(Catechism of the Catholic Church)

"The power of Satan is, nonetheless, not infinite. He is only a creature, powerful from the fact that he is pure spirit, but still a creature. He cannot prevent the building up of God's reign"[12]
(Catechism of the Catholic Church)

"An examination of conscience must also consider the reception given to the Council, this great gift of the Spirit the Church at the end of the second millennium. To what extent has the Word of God become more fully the soul of theology and the inspiration of the whole of Christian living as Dei Verbum sought?"[13]
(Pope John Paul, II)

✞✞✞✞✞

The Reality of Satan

Sacred scripture, particularly in the New Testament, gives clear evidence of the existence of the devil. In the *Fundamentals of Catholic Dogma*, Dr. Ludwig Ott writes,

"The devil possesses a certain dominion over mankind by reason of Adam's sin. This is a defined truth (de fide) from the Council of Trent, which results as a consequence of Adam's sin in the subjection to the power of the devil. (Denziger 788, 793) The Church's belief finds liturgical expression in the Ceremony of Baptism."[14]

Magisterium of the Church

The word "devil" or "Satan" does not appear in the Nicene-Constantinopolitan Creed. However, this creed which we recite at Mass each Sunday tells us that "God is Creator of all things visible and invisible." In the Council of Braga 561, the Church taught "There are not two co-eternal and opposed principles." In 1215, the fourth Lateran Council declared that the devil is not divine as the Catharist's and Bogomiles asserted. The Council of Florence and of Trent make various references to the devil.

The Second Vatican Council

The Second Vatican Council, which Pope John Paul II tells us was the way the Holy Spirit was preparing us for the year 2000, has a wealth of information on the demonic. If you read carefully the "Examination of Conscience" of Pope John Paul II, we can answer simply that one of the major reasons the Second Vatican Council did not have the spiritual impact upon the Church which we all hoped it would have, is due in no small measure to the power and influence of Satan.

As a young priest I was stunned to read of Paul VI's statement that "The smoke of Satan is within the Vatican itself."

Yet, today you read of parishes headed by priests who believe Satan is simply a medieval invention or anachronism. Anyone who has heard Fr. Paqua or

Jeannette Benkovic speak on the "New Age Movement" recognizes that Satan has attacked the Catholic Church both from within as well as from without.

The purpose of this chapter is simply to recognize that some of the evil that exists in the Church today is due to Satanic power or influence. At a time when there are priests who deny Satan's existence and question the true presence of Christ in the Eucharist, there is a proliferation of "black Masses." Satanists use a consecrated host to mock the Catholic Mass and the Eucharist.

In our parish we have had the Eucharist spirited out of the Church before an usher could make sure that the host had been consumed. Our archbishop Francis Schulte requested that ushers stand at the front near the altar to make sure that the consecrated host is not desecrated.

In one of the saddest days of my life, I had to deal with the situation of an eighth grade student in our parochial school who took a consecrated host and threw it on the floor of our Evangelization building. In tracking the culprit down, the principal learned that in the past year this student had taken the Eucharist at Mass, palmed it in his hand and thrown it into a garbage can. Suffice it to say, he did not graduate from our school.

The Teaching Of Second Vatican Council

The Second Vatican Council refers to the demonic on numerous occasions. Satan appears in five different documents. The following are quotes from each of these documents.

✞✞✞✞✞

Satan In The Ecclesiastical Magisterium[15]

Lumen Gentium: Dogmatic Constitution of the Church
There are seven references to Satan in Lumen Gentium.
They can be found in articles 6, 16, 17, 35, 48, 55 and 63.
In article 63 the church fathers wrote regarding Mary: "She
was the new Eve, who put her absolute trust not in the
ancient serpent but in God's messenger."

*Sacrosanctum Concilium: Constitution on the Sacred
Liturgy*
(Art. 6):   Just as Christ was sent by the Father, so also
he sent the apostles, filled with the Holy Spirit. This He did
so that, by preaching the Gospel to every creature, they
might proclaim that the Son of God, by his death and
resurrection, has freed us from the power of Satan, and
from death, and brought us into the kingdom of his Father.

*Gaudium et Spes: Pastoral Constitution on the Church in
the Modern World*
There are four references to Satan in this Vatican document.
They can be found in articles 2, 13, 22 and 37. In article 22
the church says: "... As an innocent lamb He merited life for
us by the free shedding of His own blood. In Him God
reconciled us, to Himself and among ourselves. From the
bondage to the devil and sin, He delivered us ..."

Ad Gentes: On the Missions
There are three references to the evil one in articles 3, 9 and
14. In article 3 of this Vatican II document we are told: "...
He sent His Son clothed in our flesh, in order that through
this Son He might snatch men from the power of darkness
and of Satan ..."

Dignitatis Humanae: On Religious Freedom
(Art. 11):   ... And they preached the Word of God in
the full confidence that there was resident in this Word itself
a divine power able to destroy all the forces arrayed against
God and to bring men to faith in Christ and to His service.

✠✠✠✠✠

Interview with Fr. Gabriele Amorth[16]

Father Gabriele Amorth, exorcist for the Diocese of
Rome, tells of a new phenomenon; that Rome, Bologna and
Turin are now the capitals of Satanic sects. According to
the magazine *30days*, members of a group called "Satan's
Chosen" gave away banknotes worth $30.00 each to people
on the street, "in the name of the devil." The sect gave
away nearly $2,000.00 in one month to attract attention.
Black masses were said by members of the Satanic sects
using hosts stolen from Catholic Churches. The heart of a
goat wrapped in a red cloth, which is a sign of nocturnal
Satanic rite, was found among the graves of Verano. The
Interior Ministry issued a warning to all police prefects in
Rome to control the activities of Satanic sects. The Interior
Ministry stated: "We are investigating 366 organizations."
He also "claims that about one in every 100 Italians has
contact with magic and esoteric sects, many of which are
associated with Devil worship."

Fr. Amorth explains the causes for the increase in
Satanic activity in Italy; "more and more people are
practicing spiritism or joining Satanic sects. It's like a
fashion, almost. ... The devil is not an impersonal entity.
This is not just a name psychoanalysts use for the abstract
ills that exist in society. He is a real person and, as Saint
Peter says in his first letter, 'like a roaring lion he is on the
prowl for someone to devour.'"

Fr. Amorth blames a poor form of theology as having spread an abstract concept of the Devil within the Catholic Church. "Yet" Fr. Amorth says, "this is the exact opposite of Gospel teaching, of the Magisterium and of the feelings of the Christian people." He continues by stating that, "many bishops don't believe that he exists either." As a result of the failure of the church to teach the reality of Satan, Satanic sects now abound in Italy. "The Catholic hierarchy is also greatly responsible for the spread of this phenomenon," Fr. Amorth claimed.

"What are the evils and maleficence you mentioned earlier?" Fr. Amorth was asked.

"There are two types: *demonic infestation and demonic possession.*" Fr. Amorth answered. "*Infestation* is provoked by a demon 'outside' the person and every now and then it assails the person causing physical and mental disturbances totally immune to medical treatment. *Possession,* which is very rare, happens 'inside' the person who is penetrated by a demon which sometimes acts using the person's own faculties. I would stress that cases of authentic demonic possession are very rare and cannot be compared with the cases of people in need of psychiatric help, ... The majority of cases I treat are cases of demonic infestation." the Roman exorcist testifies.

Fr. Amorth gives a major cause for the demonic activity as seances and membership in Satanic sects. According to one survey 36% of Italian school children have held seances. The Ouija board is an example of this type of demonic activity. Fr. Amorth mentions evil being done to another as a form of the Satanic. The evil eye, curses or voodoo rites are manifestations of the Satanic and are extremely difficult to combat. Satan himself seems to attach some extraordinary holy people like St. John Bosco, the Cure of Ars and Padre Pio in a profound way. St. Paul himself speaks of being tormented by a messenger of Satan.

Paul writes: "... I was given a thorn in the flesh, a messenger from Satan to batter me."

Asked if he feared the Devil, Fr. Amorth replied, "That beast should be afraid of me because I have the power to cast him out in Christ's name."

In the Sacrament of Baptism the church uses a prayer of exorcism. When the church authoritatively asks in the name of Jesus Christ that a person or object be protected against the power of the evil one, it is called exorcism. Outside of Baptism, a solemn exorcism can be performed **only by a priest** with the permission of the bishop. According to the new Catechism, "before an exorcism is performed, it is important to ascertain that one is dealing with the presence of the Evil One, and not an illness." By virtue of Baptism, every Christian has power over Satan by calling on the name of Jesus Christ, but not the authority to perform solemn exorcises.

✟✟✟✟✟

There were two stories that recently appeared in the news that demonstrated the power of Satan. In a fashionable area of Baton Rouge a sixteen year old adolescent shot and killed his mother. He, then, attempted to murder his father, first by shooting him and then repeatedly stabbing his dad.

The news cameraman focused on the sixteen year old as he was being arrested. He had a weird grin on his face. As the police led him away you could notice he was wearing a cross, but the cross was upside down. The reporter said this was a sign that the young man was a "Satanist."

They interviewed a friend who confirmed that the sixteen year old was involved in Satanism. "But it really wasn't that serious," he offered, "just a few harmless signs ..."

The second story happened about the same time. Three young men, ages fifteen and sixteen, were involved in a ritualistic murder of a young woman in California. They attacked, raped and killed a young woman fifteen years old. "We needed to kill a virgin," they explained, "in order to get a ticket straight to hell."

Parents who don't monitor their children's music, access to the internet or games such as "Dungeons and Dragons" or the use of a Ouija board are leaving their children open to the influence of the Satanic.

✞✞✞✞✞

Father Emile LaFranz

Fr. LaFranz was involved in the Charismatic movement in New Orleans for 25 years. He was also a classmate of mine and for a brief time my spiritual director. Fr. LaFranz recommended the following prayers to be said by priests. Fr. Emile, as he was known to charismatics around the country, died last year. I am sure that Emile is praying for us now. I have asked for a "double portion of his spirit" so that anything I might write in this book will be a help to my fellow priests who so often seem frightened when dealing with problems we were never trained to handle. Fr. LaFranz suggested the following prayers to be used by priests in the deliverance ministry.

Prayer to St. Michael

Saint Michael the Archangel,
Defend us in battle,
Be our protection against the wickedness and snares of the devil;
May God rebuke him, we humbly pray;
And do thou, O Prince of the heavenly host,
By the power of God, thrust into hell Satan and all evil spirits
Who wander through the world seeking the ruin of souls.
Amen.

Prayer to Take Authority
from Father LaFranz

In the name of Jesus, I take authority and I bind all powers and forces in the air, in the ground, in the water, in the underground, in the nether world, in nature and in fire.

You are the Lord over the entire universe and I give You the glory for Your creation. In Your name I bind all demonic forces that have come against us and our families and I seal all of us in the protection of Your Precious Blood that was shed for us on the cross. Mary, our mother, we seek your protection and intercession with the Sacred Heart of Jesus for us and our families, and surround us with your mantle of love to discourage the enemy.

St. Michael and our guardian angels, come defend us and our families in battle against all the evil ones that roam the earth.

In the name of Jesus, I bind and command all the powers and forces of evil to depart right now away from us, our homes and our lands. And we thank You Lord Jesus for You are a faithful and compassionate God. Amen.

(Note: Speak with authority when saying this prayer. Otherwise it is meaningless! Say it twice a day, once in the morning and once in the late afternoon or early evening.)

Binding Prayer

In the name of Jesus Christ, by the power of His Blood, in the authority of His Word given to me as a Christian, I bind and reject you, Satan. I command you to leave and I seal this room, my house, all the members of my family, relatives and possessions in the Blood of Jesus Christ.

I bind and send to Jesus all familiar spirits, all cardinal spirits, all spirits of affliction.

I bind and reject all the spirits in the air, in the wind, in the fire, in the nether world; in the elements, all the satanic forces of nature,

I bind and reject and send to Jesus all spirits of confusion, spirits of division, spirits of fear, spirits of disbelief, spirits of disobedience, spirits of rebellion, spirits of anger.

I command that there will be no communication between the spirits here, and I send them to Jesus.

In the name of our Lord Jesus Christ:

I break and dissolve every curse on my family, every spell, hex, evil wishes, evil desires and hereditary seals.

I come against all satanic vows, pacts, satanic sacrifices and voodoo practices.

I break and dissolve in the name of Jesus, by the power of His precious Blood, through the cross of Jesus, all links with astrologers, mediums, occult seers, satanic cults, fortune tellers, seances, Ouija boards, tarot cards, occult games of any sort.

Come, Holy Spirit, fill this room from corner to corner, ceiling to floor.

St. Michael, St. Gabriel, St. Raphael, and all the Archangels, come and fight this battle with me and for me.

I ask all the holy angels, dominations, powers, thrones, principalities to be my shield, my defense against all evil spirits.

I ask this in the name of our Lord Jesus Christ, by the power of His Precious Blood, in authority of His Word given to me as a Christian.

Lord Jesus, I ask for the infilling of the Holy Spirit. Fill me. Fill all the empty spaces within me with Your peace, Your love, Your healing, and Your joy.

I ask for an increase and a release of all gifts, all the flowers and fruits of the Holy Spirit - words of wisdom, word of knowledge, faith, healing , miracles, prophecies, discernment of spirits, tongues, interpretation of tongues, deliverance, inner healing, teaching.

I ask for an increase in all the motivational gifts, especially the gift of encouragement, gift of leadership, gift of preaching, gift of joy, gift of laughter that I may use all these gifts cheerfully. Amen.

✝✝✝✝✝

Deliverance Ministry

If you are familiar with the healing ministry in fundamentalist churches you will recognize that deliverance is handled differently in the Catholic Church. Experts in the Catholic Church agree on two fundamental points:

1. In the Catholic Church most "deliverance" occurs primarily in the confessional (i.e. Sacrament of Penance.)
2. A Catholic priest should always be present whenever deliverance is done by a Catholic healing team. For example, Sister Briege McKenna, who has a wonderful healing ministry, would never pray a deliverance prayer unless she was supported and backed by a priest.

Incidentally, Fr. DeGrandis, a priest involved in deliverance ministry, has three simple rules.

1.   Lots of personal forgiveness of yourself and others.
2.   Use of the sacraments particularly the sacrament of Penance.
3.   Frequent reception of the Eucharist and adoration of the Blessed Sacrament.

Dangers in the Deliverance Ministry

Clearly, the Catholic Church recognizes the need for a trained exorcist in a diocese. But this individual, as pointed out from Canon Law must be a holy priest, delegated by the bishop and a man of prayer and fasting.

Catholic laymen on healing teams run a great risk in deliverance ministry. These risks are spelled out clearly by Cardinal Ratzinger in a document, Inde Ab Aliquot Annis, dated September 29, 1984.

✞✞✞✞✞

On the Current Norms Governing Exorcisms
Inde Ab Aliquot Annis

Issued by the Congregation for the Doctrine of the Faith on Sept. 29, 1984

Excellentissime Domine,
    For several years, in certain areas of the Church, assemblies formed to pray for liberation from the influence of demons (though they do not perform exorcisms as such) have been increasing in number. These assemblies are often led by members of the laity, even when there is a priest present.
    Since the Congregation for the Doctrine of the Faith has been asked what is the proper attitude towards these

activities, this Dicastery deems it necessary to make known to all Ordinaries the response which follows:

1. Canon 1172 of the Code of Canon Law declares that (section 1) "no one can legitimately perform exorcisms over the possessed unless he has obtained special and express permission from the local ordinary." And it decrees that (section 2) "such permission for the local ordinary is to be granted only to a presbyter endowed with piety, knowledge, prudence and integrity of life."[17] Bishops are therefore strongly urged to enforce the observance of these prescriptions.

2. It follows also from these same prescriptions that Christ's faithful may not employ the formula of exorcism against Satan and the fallen angels which is excerpted from that formula made official by order of the Supreme Pontiff Leo XIII, and certainly may not use the entire text of that exorcism. Let all bishops take care to admonish the faithful about this matter whenever such instruction is required.

3. Finally, for the same reasons, Bishops are asked to guard lest those who lack the required power attempt to lead assemblies in which prayers are employed to obtain liberation from demons, and in the course of which the demons are directly disturbed and an attempt is made to determine their identity. This applies even to cases which, although they do not involve true diabolical possession, nevertheless are seen in some way to manifest diabolical influence.

Of course, the enunciation of these norms should not stop the faithful of Christ from praying, as Jesus taught us, that they may be freed from evil (cf. Mt 6:13). Moreover, Pastors should take this opportunity to remember what the tradition of the Church teaches about the function properly assigned to the intercession of the Most Blessed Virgin

Mary, the Apostles and the Saints, even in the spiritual battle of Christians against the evil spirits.

May I take this occasion to convey my great feelings of esteem for you, remaining your servant in the Lord,

Joseph Card. Ratzinger, Prefect[18]

[1] (Pope John Paul, II, *Tertio Millennio Adveniente*, (Boston, MA.: Pauline Books & Media, 1994), page 47, #40.

[2] *Catechism of the Catholic Church*, (New York: Catholic Book Publishing Co., 1992), page 421, #1694.

[3] Pilla, Bishop Anthony, "Evangelization and Holiness: Toward the New Millennium", Page 394.

[4] (Ibid, Page 394.)

[5] (Pope John Paul, II, *Tertio Millennio Adveniente*, pages 61-62, #59.)

[6] (Ibid, page 47, #40.)

[7] (Ibid, page 48, #41.)

[8] Burkhardt, Monsignor Edward C., Synopsis of A Pilgrim's Way Bible Study on back of text.

[9] Taken from *The Denver Catholic Biblical School Program* study manual, (Paulist Press).

[10] Abbott, Walter M., *The Documents of Vatican, II*, "Dogmatic Constitution on the Church #48, (New York: The America Press, 1966), page 80.

[11] (*Catechism of the Catholic Church*, page 100, #397.)

[12] (Ibid, page 99, #395.)

[13] (Pope John Paul, II, *Tertio Millennio Adveniente*, page 42-43, #36.)

[14] Ott, Ludwig, *Fundamentals of Catholic Dogma*, page 119.

[15] (Abbott, *The Documents of Vatican, II*, #48) This information was researched by Fr. Joe Benson.

[16] Paci, Stefano M., *30Days*, "The Devil of a Fashion", (No. 1 - 1996), pages 18-21.

[17] Coriden, James A., Thomas J. Green and Donald E. Heintschel, *The Code of Canon Law: A Text and Commentary*, (New York: Paulist Press, 1985), page 826.

[18] Letter from Cardinal Joseph Ratzinger, Prefect.

MARY THE SPOUSE OF THE HOLY SPIRIT

Section Three
Year Two -- Holy Spirit and Mary,
His Spouse -- 1998

"1998, the second year of the preparatory phase, will be dedicated in a particular way to the Holy Spirit and to His sanctifying presence within the community of Christ's disciples."[1]
(Pope John Paul, II)

"The primary tasks of the preparation for the Jubilee thus include a renewed appreciation of the presence and activity of the Spirit, Who acts within the Church both in the Sacraments, especially in Confirmation, and in the variety of charisms, roles and ministries which He inspires for the good of the Church."[2]
(Pope John Paul, II)

"Mary, who conceived the Incarnate Word by the power of the Holy Spirit and then in the whole of her life allowed herself to be guided by His interior activity, will be contemplated and imitated during this year above all as the woman who was docile to the voice of the Spirit, a woman of silence and attentiveness, a woman of hope who, like Abraham accepted God's will ... and is a radiant model for those who entrust themselves with all their hearts to the promises of God."[3]
(Pope John Paul, II)

Chapter One
The Charisms of the Holy Spirit

"It cannot be denied that, for many Christians, the spiritual life is passing through a time of uncertainty which affects not only their moral life but also their life of prayer and the theological correctness of the faith. Faith, already put to the test by the challenges of our times, is sometimes disoriented by erroneous theological views, the spread of which is abetted by the crisis of obedience vis-à-vis the Church's Magisterium.
And with respect to the Church of our time, how can we not lament the lack of discernment, *which at times became even acquiescence, shown by many Christians concerning the violation of fundamental human rights by totalitarian regimes?"*[4]
(Pope John Paul, II)

"By this power of the Spirit, God's children can bear much fruit. He who has grafted us onto the true vine will make us bear 'the fruit of the spirit: ... love, joy, peace, patience, kindness, goodness, faithfulness, gentleness, self control.'
(Gal. 5:22-23) 'We live by the Spirit'; the more we renounce ourselves, the more we 'walk by the spirit'
(St. Basil, De Spiritu Sancto, 15,36: page 32,132)."[5]
(Catechism of the Catholic Church)

✟✟✟✟✟

The Charisms of the Holy Spirit

     The Holy Spirit is pouring out His gifts on every Catholic community in this country. In 1960 Pope John XXIII prayed for an outpouring of the Holy Spirit. That prayer has been answered beyond our fondest dreams. The gifts of the Holy Spirit are in evidence everywhere.

Most of the charisms of the Holy Spirit seem to some to be "ordinary." However, the role of the Holy Spirit is to be the sanctifier. If you wonder why nothing is happening in your parish, ask yourself if the Holy Spirit has been the neglected member of the Trinity.

There are three things we must do to prepare the remnant church for the outpouring of the Holy Spirit.

1. Encourage the ordinary gifts of the Holy Spirit.
2. Be open to the possibility of extraordinary gifts.
3. Learn to discern the charisms of the Holy Spirit.

The Ordinary Gifts of the Holy Spirit

A Pentecost sermon listed the major charisms of the Holy Spirit that are fostered at St. Margaret Mary; they are "ordinary gifts."

1. Become proclaimers of the Word of God (i.e., evangelizers).
2. Minister through evangelization
3. The Holy Spirit makes Jesus the "Lord of our life."
4. The Holy Spirit allows us to minister to one another.
   a. Through prayer before the Blessed Sacrament - Adoration.
   b. Through Mass, daily Rosary, and intercessory prayer.
5. Minister to our own families -- teach children the meaning of "carrying the cross."
6 Become fully armed disciples of Jesus Christ through prayer and study.
7. Teach other children as a religion teacher.
8. Carry your own cross with courage.

✟✟✟✟✟

Pentecost Sermon

The first reading for the vigil of Pentecost is from the Book of Ezekiel 37:4-5;7. The prophet Ezekiel is led out into a field of bones to prophesy. "Dry bones, hear the word of the Lord! Thus says the Lord God to these bones: See! I will bring spirit into you, that you may come to life."

"I prophesied," he continued, "as I had been told, and even as I was prophesying I heard a noise; it was a rattling as the bones came together, bone joining bone."

My brothers and sisters, the Lord is calling this community to come alive. He wants to take our dry bones and breath life into them. He wants you to be among the remnant community during the Day of the Lord. It must be the Holy Spirit that breathes life into us. However, He expects us to do our part.

Jesus gave us the reason so many churches are made up of dry bones. Jesus, as He prepared for His departure from the world, made this prayer: "... Father ... I do not ask that you take them out of the world, but to guard them from the evil one."

Jesus was concerned that the evil one, the devil, would entrap us. Yet, there are many today who do not even believe in the devil.

There are many in our community who are dry bones because the power of evil has enticed them. I believe the warnings of Our Blessed Mother about the punishments to come involve addictions.

Satan has entrapped many through casual use of drugs. The 25 million Americans who use drugs, even marijuana, are responsible for the deaths that occur from Harlem to Los Angeles. They are in Satan's service. They are dry bones that may never come alive.

There are many who serve the evil one through their inability to free themselves from addictions to food, alcohol and sex. There are ten million alcoholics in this country. They no longer have any control. Yet they continue to destroy their family without seeking help. They serve Satan's cause.

Many refuse to teach their children to say no to themselves. They allow their little ones to languish before TV for hours on end. They become couch potatoes and stuff their faces with food. It is a poor substitute for love. Their children will find it difficult to say no to sex and drugs. This will be because as parents some of you failed to teach them to say no to themselves in small matters like food and TV. You are dry bones that need to come to life.

The answer to these complex issues is the Holy Spirit. In the Acts of the Apostles, the Holy Spirit, the third person of the Trinity, appeared to the apostles as tongues of fire. Through his power he changed these weak, fearful apostles. He filled them with his spirit and they became **Proclaimers of the Word of God.** The Holy Spirit alone can change you and me. He can bring us back to life, if we let Him.

In St. Paul's first letter to the Corinthians 12:3 he tells us that we can not even say "'Jesus is Lord,' except in the Holy Spirit."

Certainly you and I want to say that **Jesus is Lord of our Lives,** we want him to be the center of our being. However, we need the Holy Spirit. He is the sanctifier -- the one who makes holy. You received the Holy Spirit, first in Baptism. Most of you have also received the Holy Spirit through confirmation.   It is time to stir up the graces you have already received.

Paul goes on to show how the Holy Spirit expects us to act once He breathed life into these dry bones. He wants us to **minister to one another**.   Paul says in 1 Corinthians 12:7, "To each person the manifestation of the Spirit is given for the common good."   It is your responsibility to question the Holy Spirit. What do you want me to do?

All of us are called to minister through prayer. The Holy Spirit wants you to spend time before the **Blessed Sacrament**. Perhaps he wants you to attend daily Mass or recite the rosary daily with members of your family. Our community has now embarked on intercessory prayer every Friday night. Prayer is a ministry.

The Holy Spirit may be calling all of you to **minister to your family**. Teach your children the value of sacrifice and self-denial. Let the little ones understand the message of Jesus, "If you wish to be my disciple you must take up your cross daily and follow me." Teach your children the importance of a generous heart, or selfishness will rule their lives. Your children need to minister to your parents.

The Holy Spirit may be calling you to proclaim the word through **evangelization**. Have you ever invited a non-Catholic, a fallen-away Catholic, or an unchurched person to join us at St. Margaret Mary? There are 80 million unchurched in the United States alone. St. James gives us a good reason for this ministry. "Remember this:" he says, "The person who brings a sinner back from his way will save his soul from death and cancel a multitude of sins." (James 5:20)

Participate in the evangelization program. The Holy Spirit is calling each of you to be "fully armed disciples of Jesus Christ." In September, 1995, we began with 300 committed adults. We asked them to disciple one person a year for four years. In the second semester we had 430 adults. We need a minimum of 600 adults to sign up for the 1996-97 sessions. If we double each year we will have 5000 "fully armed disciples of Jesus Christ" by the year 2000. Ask the Holy Spirit to turn your "dry bones" into a testimony of knowledge and love for Jesus Christ. Sanctification is His forte.

Perhaps the Holy Spirit is asking you to **minister to others through teaching**. What the Holy Spirit wants are laymen and laywomen willing to share their love of Jesus with his little ones. We will never become a remnant community until we take care of all the needs of the children.

"All of us have been given to drink of the one spirit," Paul tells us. Are you unwilling to share your love of Jesus because you are too busy or don't care? Are you dry bones that need to be revived?

A recovering drug addict and alcoholic told this story. He had used drugs and alcohol for twelve and a half years. He decided to go into F. Edward Hebert Hospital for rehabilitation. Once there he was filled with self pity.

One day riding on the elevator with him was a young woman completely paralyzed. One side of her face was untouched. It was obvious she had been a very beautiful woman. The other side was grotesque because of the paralysis. 'Yet,' he said, 'she smiled at me.' His whole life changed. He was on the road to recovery. All because a young woman, bearing an unbelievable cross, ministered to him by smiling. The Holy Spirit is calling each of you to minister to one another. When that happens these dry bones will come to life. The Holy Spirit will truly make our community come alive; a vast army serving Jesus as Lord.

✝✝✝✝✝

Be Open to the Extraordinary Gifts of the Holy Spirit

For the last two years the main speakers at the Catholic Charismatic Conference in New Orleans have had the gift of healing. In 1995 Fr. Tardiff was the feature speaker. In 1996 it was Fr. Matthew Naikomphrambil, a priest from India.

There have been extraordinary healings at both Charismatic Conferences. Unfortunately there is a reluctance on the part of many priests even to acknowledge the possibility that the Holy Spirit would give this charism of healing to the church today.

I believe that the Holy Spirit is working in every Christian Church today. It should come as no surprise to find charisms of the Holy Spirit in other denominations. The sad fact is that the Catholic Church has lost many members to fundamentalists, particularly Pentecostals. This is because of a reluctance on the part of some priests, to accept the possibility that extraordinary charisms of the Holy Spirit might occur in their parishes.

✝✝✝✝✝

Testimony of Dottie

"On Saturday, April 1, 1995, at the Catholic Charismatic Conference in New Orleans, Fr. Tardiff received word that someone was present who had lost a close member of their family to suicide. Fr. Tardiff said that this family member is in Heaven. He said, "Rest assured that this person is in Heaven because at the moment of his death he repented." Fr. Tardiff further said that as a sign from God so that you will know there will be a healing in your legs. Immediately our teenage daughter turned to me and said, "Mom, he's talking to you." My husband also turned to me and said, "Dottie, he's talking about you." A close friend of ours, Johnnie Hernandez, also turned to me and said, "Dottie, you know he's talking about you." Almost two years earlier on June 21, 1993, my brother, Roby committed suicide.

"After Fr. Tardiff's talk, our friend Johnnie told me that during Father's talk he (Johnnie) attempted to pray for his two sisters who are in poor health. However, he was unable to because he kept seeing in his mind an image of my mother, my other brother, and me. Johnnie said that we were very happy and were smiling. Johnnie said that as soon as Fr. Tardiff stated that the person who had committed suicide was in Heaven, but before Father stated what the sign would be, he prayed that God would heal the pain in my legs as a sign to me if it were my brother Roby about whom Fr. Tardiff had received word.

"I have suffered from **constant, severe** pain in my legs for years; beginning when I was just a teenager. I inherited extremely bad varicose veins, broken veins, and poor circulation from my paternal grandmother. My legs hurt seven days a week, 24 hours a day. Frequently at night the pain even made it difficult for me to fall asleep.

"Following my brother's death I made the decision to **embrace** the pain in my legs and offer my suffering to God. I hoped that God would have mercy on my brother Roby's soul and let him enter the Kingdom of Heaven. This was so that he would finally have the peace, love and joy of Christ that he never had during his earthly life.

"At one of our regular prayer group praise gatherings **before** my healing, I shared with Johnnie how his offering of the pain in his knees for the lost souls in Purgatory had inspired me to embrace the pain in my legs, (instead of wishing that I didn't have the pain) and offer the suffering for Roby's soul.

"Prior to his death, Roby was experiencing depression and the breakup of his marriage. Roby lived in Denham Springs but he would call me and we would have long talks over the phone. I tried to encourage him. I told Roby how merciful and loving Jesus is and how much Jesus loved him. Roby judged that he was too terrible of a sinner for God to accept him and unworthy of God's love. I told Roby about the **Divine Mercy of Jesus** and how it was his for the asking. All he had to do was ask. God had placed it in my heart to tell him about the Divine Mercy of Jesus and emphasize His love and compassion for **all**, especially sinners (all of us) and those most in need of His mercy and compassion. My brother loved God, but he was ill and carried many wounds of the heart from childhood. I believe that he remembered my words, however; and at the moment of his death, reached out for the mercy of God.

"After my brother's death, I prayed faithfully the Chaplet of Divine Mercy for my brother's soul, begging Our Lord's mercy. For more than a year and a half I prayed. Shortly before the Catholic Charismatic Conference in 1995, I was home alone spending my day in prayer. I cried out to God, that if He didn't mind, would He please let me know where my brother's soul was. I also told God that if He didn't choose to reveal that to me I would accept his will. Afterwards, I didn't give my request any more thought.

"When Fr. Tardiff received word from God about my brother, I knew in my heart that it was me to whom he was speaking. However, my awareness of my own unworthiness made me reluctant to claim and proclaim this gift of healing and mercy at the conference.

"I did go to my priests, Fr. Richard Carroll and Fr. Joe Benson at St. Margaret Mary and told them about the

Divine Mercy healing of my brother's soul and my legs. It has been a year and there is still NO pain in my legs. I have also given testimony to others of this tremendous grace. Jesus Christ has blessed me and my family with his infinite mercy and compassion and He has called me to witness to others of His mercy and infinite love. Praise God! Praise the Divine Mercy of Jesus! Jesus, I trust in you!"

Chapter Two
The Gift of Our Lady

"Christ the redeemer of the world, is the one Mediator between God and men, and there is no other name under heaven by which we can be saved." (cf. Acts 4:12)[6]
(Pope John Paul, II)

"The affirmation of the central place of Christ cannot therefore be separated from the recognition of the role played by His Most Holy Mother. Veneration of her, when properly understood can in no way take away from the 'dignity and efficacy of Christ the one Mediator.' Mary in fact constantly points to her Divine Son and She is proposed to all believers as the model of faith which is put into practice."[7]
(Pope John Paul, II)

✝✝✝✝✝

The Gift

I underwent a life-threatening operation in October, 1995. I returned to offer Mass for the first time at the 4 p.m. Vigil of Christmas.

I was keenly aware of the gift of life that had been given to me. My left vocal cord was paralyzed, and I could barely speak above a whisper. However, I realized that for some reason, through the intercession of Our Lady, I was still alive.

Christmas, 1995, I was able to focus on the major gift that God the Father has given all of us -- His Son Jesus Christ as our savior and redeemer.

I was also aware of the deep debt I owed Our Blessed Mother. By nature I am a fearful person. Yet, despite this life-threatening surgery I was unafraid; I knew Mary was at my side.

In my prayer time Our Lady spoke directly to my heart; "As long as I am near you, you have nothing to fear." I believe this message is meant not only for me and our community at St. Margaret Mary, it is meant for you, my dear reader. Proper devotion to Mary always brings us to Jesus, her Son and our Redeemer.

Finally, my Christmas talk allowed me to focus on my personal gift from Our Lady - the love of my children, especially little girls. The greatest sacrifice of the priesthood for me was not the vow not to marry or the sense of loneliness that accompanies this promise. I have always found the priesthood to be a richly rewarding life. Yet, I have always longed to have my own little daughters. Our Lady made it quite clear to me that her special relationship with me can be seen by the spiritual children I call my own. Whenever I would get on a pity party, Mary would remind me... "Tell me again, what did you say you wanted most in life?"

Of course Mary knew it wasn't money or friends or even fame or success. I only asked for little girls, and she has brought the smiles and tears and prayers of some of God's most precious children into my life. These "little girls" range in age from infancy to eighty.

✠✠✠✠✠

Christmas Sermon - 1995

Tonight, as we celebrate Christmas, the Catholic Church calls us to remember an extraordinary gift we have all received. Sacred scripture tells us God the Father so loved the world that He sent His own Son to give us eternal life. The Christmas season has become one of the most stressful for many families. For in trying to find the perfect gift, they overlook the great treasure that is theirs for the asking.

Before I tell you of the great treasure you can possess, I would like to tell you what has happened to me in the past two months. This will help you to see what Our Blessed Mother is trying to teach us.

For four years I have had individuals who would come up and tell me they had seen a vision of me hanging on a cross. At the Confirmation last year, two men separately in a vision saw me shot and killed during the Confirmation ceremony.

My recent heart condition necessitated surgery. When I was told of the dangers of my heart surgery, i.e. and acute aortic dissection, I was not frightened. Somehow, I knew beyond a shadow of a doubt that my work wasn't finished. I knew I would be protected by Our Blessed Mother.

Despite an excellent medical team led by Dr. Tom Hall, internist, Dr. Echenique, heart specialist, and Dr. Gregory Groglio, heart surgeon, I was at great physical risk.

Seven weeks after the surgery, Dr. Groglio released me. This young physician did a great job in this seven hour surgery. Dr. Hernandez, the anesthesiologist, tells me that just before the surgery I asked the medical team to join hands in prayer. I am sure your prayers were with this marvelous medical team. On January 12, I will have minor surgery by Dr. Bob Miller at Tulane University Hospital, which is expected to partially restore my voice.

The days following my initial surgery were grace-filled for me as Our Blessed Mother spoke to my heart. No,

I am not a visionary or an inner locutionist, but Our Lady gave me a gift.

The gift Our Lady gave me was to be one of her "priest intercessors." That means we have a special relationship. "There is no way I can ever turn down a request that I know comes from your heart for your community, she told me. "On the other hand, you must always say yes to any request that I make of you....even if it means giving up your life. You are one of my priest intercessors."

Incidentally, a few days after I returned to the rectory, I received a book written about Christina Gallagher, a visionary from Ireland. This is what Christine says about priest-intercessors, "The meaning of the priesthood is to be a victim in union with Jesus: priests share in a special way in the victimhood of Christ, the Great High Priest Who is sacrificed for the sins of the world. The priests who are enduring the purification process will, therefore, experience emptiness during and following it, because the benefits will be applied by God to the souls whom they pasture in their shepherding of God's flock. Jesus pastures His sheep by means of the priest's ministry. So priests will be benefiting the flock in their charge in a deeply spiritual way, as they themselves are led closer to perfection..."[8]

✝✝✝✝✝

Mary's Contract - the Willingness to Surrender

A mother recently told the story of bringing her daughter home after the daughter had given up her new born child for adoption. The 19 year old sobbed bitterly; her grief uncontrollable. The mother felt her heart literally breaking in two.

I could understand this because for many years my heart has been torn apart. Many of my children have left the church. Over a dozen of my most precious children have committed suicide. I prayed to Our Lady, but somehow my prayers never seemed to be heard. One day Our Lady, by her intercession, allowed one of my children who had attempted suicide to live.

It was Mary's Christmas gift to me. From that moment we had a deal ... she would bring my requests for my community to Jesus. I am to do whatever She asks of me, even if it means spending time in the hospital.

The Gift

Our Lady made it quite clear that each of you, my children, will be offered a gift - to be sheltered and protected in her heart during the coming tribulations - the same way she protected me during my major heart surgery. Many of you have done everything Our Lady asked you to do to become a Remnant Church -- to spend time in adoration of the Blessed Sacrament, to love Our Lady with a deep and abiding love, and to teach our children to love Our Mother. You have been loyal to the Holy Father. You have found repentance through the Divine Mercy of Jesus Christ. You have opened yourself to the power of the Holy Spirit. Now she is offering you the gift of her protection during the time of chastisement.

The Price of the Gift

The gift of protection by Our Lady will be yours provided Jesus Christ truly is Lord of your life. After communion we will all make a public commitment to Jesus as Lord. This is our community gift to Jesus our Savior.

✞✞✞✞✞

Freedom from Fear

Everything leads us to believe the time of tribulation predicted in *Revelation* is close at hand. The gift we offer at St. Margaret Mary is the protection that could come only from Jesus Christ. After all of these years, Jesus is never able to say no to his mother.

My heart surgery was a symbol. My heart has been broken by the pain I experienced by the loss of faith of my children; but the heart has been repaired, and my voice will return.

The same protection Mary gave to me in my time of trial, is yours for the asking. You and your family will be guarded in the Immaculate Heart of Mary during the coming chastisements. The treasure you have will be a **freedom from fear**. Mary, Our Mother will protect you during these trials. However, her protection comes at a price. For her priest-intercessors, the price is suffering and humiliation. For the rest it is simply to make Jesus the Lord of your life.

To accomplish this you need adoration, discipleship and structured prayer and study. In short to be a fully armed disciple of Jesus Christ, one who can say Jesus is my Lord!

Recognizing the Gift

Bill Bright, the head of Campus Crusade tells a wonderful story in his video, "Witnessing Without Fear". During the depression a family was nearly destitute. Their farm land seemed to be worthless. They couldn't grow anything on it. In desperation they were close to selling the worthless land and moving out of Texas.

Shortly before they sold the property, they were offered money for oil leases. It turned out that this worthless land had an enormous amount of crude oil. It became one of the largest producing wells in Texas. In a short time the family that was at the doorsteps of poverty became immensely wealthy.[9]

That family discovered the gift of God the Father in time. They found oil and wealth. As Christians we have been given an even greater gift by our heavenly Father. We have been given Jesus Christ as our Lord and Savior. We have been given Mary, the Mother of Jesus, as our spiritual mother, our intercessor.

In my life I have also been given a very small gift. I asked Our Lady, when I was in the hospital, why I wasn't given some of the great gifts that the Holy Spirit is passing out today such as the gift of healing. Our Lady told me, "you were given the gift you most needed as a priest - to be an intercessor." It's not that I am great at praying. In fact I am sure my guardian angel complains whenever I visit the Blessed Sacrament Chapel, and start saying my breviary. "Here comes the mumbler," he groans. But in God's plan, suffering is a form of intercession, and Our Lady has helped me to become childlike enough to try to get my spiritual children to do whatever she thinks will help them be prepared for the "Triumph of the Immaculate Heart of Mary" and the return of Jesus Christ.

Will your community be ready? Suppose the tribulation predicted in the *Book of Revelation* takes place in your lifetime; how will you handle it? Make Jesus Christ the Lord of your life and His mother, Mary, will protect you and your family through personal trials as well as the tribulation. "As long as I am at your side, you have nothing to fear," is Mary's promise to you.

Chapter Three
Obstacles to the Holy Spirit

Obstacle One
Lack of Discernment
Confusion Concerning Visionaries

There is a need on the part of Bishops and Pastors to discern the use of the charisms of the Holy Spirit in a diocese or in a parish. Bill Reck, President of the Riehle Foundation, is authoring a book now ready for relase (the summer of 1996), titled *Dear Marian Movement: Let God be God.* The book exposes some of the pitfalls in the current craze of claimed visionaries who threaten the Marian Movement.

Bill makes the point that local Bishops need to prudently begin their discernment at the early stages. However, what sometimes happens is the local Bishop will disapprove a visionary and an imprimatur will be secured elsewhere. The Marian Movement has been a great defense against the attacks of Satan. However, the evil one has infiltrated this movement by "false visionaries." Great discernment is needed today to protect the authentic messages given by Our Blessed Mother.

The Discernment of Pastors

On the local level most priests given the power of Holy Orders can discern the issues that affect their own community. Recognizing the authority given to the pastor by the Catechism of the Catholic Church, all charisms of the Holy Spirit are subject to pastoral authority. However, it is also important that the pastor not try to stifle the work of the Holy Spirit.

One of the charismatic leaders from Picayune, Mississippi told me two wonderful stories. The first was that of the Irish priest who decided he could "regulate the Holy Spirit." This pastor had prayer teams who would pray over people after Mass. However, he did not want anyone "slain in the spirit." This expression sometimes called "resting in the Spirit," is a powerful experience for some. After being prayed over they gently fall backwards. Usually there are "catchers" who allow the persons to fall backwards without hurting themselves.

The Irish pastor had given the instruction that no one would be allowed to "rest in the Spirit." One of the prayer teams made up completely of ordinary parishioners, without one charismatic among them, began to pray over those who came forward. All of a sudden everyone coming forward was being "slain in the Spirit" by this particular prayer team. "I guess there is no way I can regulate the Holy Spirit," the Irish priest lamented.

The other story involved a priest who came to a prayer meeting dressed in his non-clerical clothes. He came incognito. This priest, dressed as a layman, came in late and went up to be prayed over by the prayer team.

As the lay person was about to anoint the priest he saw a huge hand in front of the priest. The layman heard a clear voice say to him, "Do not anoint the one whom I have already anointed." Incidentally the oil blessed for this ceremony is not the oil of the sick, nor do laymen give the sacrament of the anointing of the sick is sometimes called the "last rites." This sacrament is administered by a priest.

"Are you a priest?" the shaken layman asked the disguised priest.

"Yes, I am," he replied.

"The Holy Spirit does not want us to anoint you," the layman said.

Two Simple Rules of Discernment

1. The individual who exercises a charism must have humility. Whatever gift you have is given not for your own glory, but given for the building up of the Body of Christ. This is clear from the Catechism of the Catholic Church.

> *"It is in this sense that discernment of charisms is always necessary. No charism is exempt from being referred and submitted to the Church's shepherds. 'Their office (is) not indeed to extinguish the Spirit, but to test all things and hold fast to what is good,' (1 Thess. 5:12, 19-21) so that all the diverse and complementary charisms work together for 'the common good'*
> *(1 Cor. 12:7)"[10]*
> *(Catechism of the Catholic Church)*

"By your fruits you will know them." If the person gifted by the Holy Spirit believes these gifts are a sign of personal holiness; they can deceive themselves. The individual will begin to feel that they are vessels of grace instead of a simple channel. They lack humility.

2. Every charism must be under the authority of the pastor in his parish. Discord can occur unless the pastor is kept informed and the gifts are administered under his authority.

Discernment - How do I know if this is of God

One of the truly anointed speakers I met at the Philadelphia Conference was Fr. Bill McCarthy, M.S.S.A. Fr. McCarthy is a scripture scholar and co-founder of "My

Father's House" in Moodus, CT. (203) 873-1581. He is a leader in the Charismatic, Cursillo and Marian Movements. He is also involved in the healing ministry and gives parish retreats and missions.

Fr. McCarthy answers one of the most difficult questions of our times, "How can I tell if something is coming from the Spirit of God?"

Fr. McCarthy points out that there are certain realities over which all discernment is placed:

1: God our Father has a wonderful plan for His people.
2. That this loving Father is covenanted to watch over, guide, nurture and protect His people.
3. This loving covenanted plan is realized most fully in the person of Jesus, His Son whom the Father sent as the way, truth and the life.
4. That Jesus left His Spirit to guide His body the Church.
5. The Spirit speaks through the Church, the Bible, signs, Sacraments, apparitions, events, persons, experiences, Etc. He also speaks through our thoughts, our deepest feelings, dreams, visions and intuition of each member of the church personally and to the church as a whole.
6. The final certainty lies with the whole church whom the spirit protects from substantial error.

Nine Rules of Discernment

In discernment, Fr. McCarthy says there are certain principles for individual discernment.

1. When I seek God with all my heart I will find him (Jeremiah31:34). When one is ready to die to self

and seek only God, nine-tenths of the problems are overcome.

2. I seek the will of God as revealed by the Church and by the Spirit. The inspiration, the teachings of the church and the scriptures must be in line. What is of God will always be consistent with the Church and the Scriptures.
3. Take into account providential circumstances that will often point in one direction.
4. Seek wise counsel from a spiritual director or wise friend in the Lord.
5. Be willing to fast
6. Look to the fruit. "By their fruits you shall know them."
7. Expect harassments and difficulties for Satan will not stand by idle.
8. Expect deep inner peace and joy despite the struggle.
9. Be willing to wait for doors to open.

Fr. McCarthy concludes his article on discernment by saying:
"When the idea/event is not of God,
    God says no
When you are not right, God says grow
When the time is not right, God says slow
When everything is right, God says GO!"

"If you really want to know what God wants you to do, simply ask Him. Make sure you really expect a solid answer for a double-minded person will be unsettled as a wave in the sea." (James 1:5-6)[11]

Fr. Bill McCarthy graciously shared his insights in discernment. I would particularly recommend Bill for his Life in the Spirit Seminars and his conference and healing missions.

✞✞✞✞✞

Obstacle Two
Lack of Humility
Humility -- A Key to the Outpouring of the Holy Spirit

As we prepare for the Third Millennium and the Triumph of the Immaculate Heart of Mary, we need to recognize the importance of the gift of humility. Scripture tells us "whoever exalts himself shall be humbled, but whoever humbles himself shall be exalted." (Matthew 23:12) It is clear from the life of Our Blessed Mother that she perfectly modeled both humility and love. We cannot ignore these virtues if we wish to have the power of the Holy Spirit operating in our Catholic Parishes.

Humility is the key to unlocking the gifts of the Holy Spirit in an individual or in a community.

What is humility? Humility is a virtue that allows us to become like little children, to have a sense of awe about God, to recognize our own gifts but never forget that they come from God the Father; to know that we are sinners but we are free because of Divine Mercy; to never forget that we are children of God the Father Who loves us; and we are temples of the Holy Spirit.

Humility Allows Us to Become like Little Children

Jesus said, "I assure you, unless you change and become like little children, you will not enter the kingdom of God." (Matthew 18:3)

Children have a sense of awe, an awareness that God can do anything. I believe that is happening in our community: A number of individuals are becoming aware of the presence of God. This child-like attitude manifests itself in reverence and worship. You can feel the presence of God in the worship and singing. You know you are on "Holy Ground."

This child-like attitude has allowed a number of individuals to see manifestations of Jesus, Our Lady and angels. In most communities, they would be ridiculed. In this community we accept the premise that if you become like a little child, God Our Father will open your heart to His gifts, especially the Holy Spirit.

God Manifests His Presence in Many Ways

If God wishes He can manifest His presence through joy, tears, or a sense of love. If he wants he can even use mental images. St. Paul, writing to the Hebrews (12:18-22) said: "You have not drawn near to an untouchable mountain. ... No, you have drawn near to ... the heavenly Jerusalem, (i.e. a sense of Church) to myriad's of angels in festal gathering...to God the Judge of all...."

An example of this happened recently. Father Benson, my associate pastor, was confronted with a dilemma. Father Benson prayed, "Break open my heart to discern."

After Mass two people came to see him. The first said, "I saw a heart split in two with the Holy Spirit over it. I don't know what it means." The second person came up to Father Joe and said, "I saw a heart open and doves fly out. Do you have any idea what it meant?"

Fr. Joe knew that the Holy Spirit was confirming his prayer by using mental images given to those two parishioners. St. Paul is correct, "we have not drawn near to an untouchable mountain."

Gifts Confirm a Childlike Message

In a recent sermon, I said, "God the Father will do anything to save His children including sending them the tribulations."

A parishioner came in after my first Mass: "On Friday night I was given a message. It took hours before I fully understood it. It was exactly what you said in the homily. 'God, the Father will do anything to save His children including sending them the tribulations.'" This was a confirmation to me. God loves His children so much, He is even willing to send the tribulations to save their souls.

Sometimes individuals experience phenomena inside the mind (interior) or as a visual image (exterior). A recent Sunday was an example of this. One parishioner saw Jesus "as Divine Mercy, with the rays of His grace flowing out. Mary was present as was St. Michael, the archangel. When Father Carroll went behind the altar I saw a vision of him on the cross."

At the same Mass another parishioner saw angels around the altar. "I also saw the hands and side of Jesus were bleeding. Our Lady was present." "There is Divine Mercy...but there is also Divine Justice," she was told.

A third individual, at the same Mass, saw a large angel standing at my back and an image of Mary. There were words written over my head, "Mercy-Justice." "Pay close attention to the Mass. This is one of my shepherds who will lead you. He has the keys."

"Jesus was standing behind Father Carroll and the rays of Divine Mercy were coming from Jesus to Father Carroll and out of the Eucharist to the congregation. The voice said, 'Through him you will know of My mercy.'"

"Later during the Mass, above the altar was a huge host. Behind the host was God the Father, on the throne."

What I found interesting was that these three parishioners saw similar things at the same Mass, all confirming the content of the sermon on Divine Mercy and the love of God the Father in giving Jesus to us as our savior and Redeemer.

Humility will Open you to the gifts of the Holy Spirit

"Conduct your affairs with humility, and you will be loved more than a giver of gifts. Humble yourself the more, the greater you are; and you will find favor with God." Sirach 3:17.

The Holy Spirit wants to work in your life if you are humble, that is, if you are like a little child.

A false humility, i.e. pride, often keeps us from the gifts of the Holy Spirit. For years I was reluctant to pray over our Confirmation class on retreat for fear they would discover I was "not spirit filled."

In any gift you receive you must recognize that you are only an instrument in the hands of God the Father. The healing ministry will become an important element in the triumph of Our Lady if we don't let fear deter us.

Our Blessed Mother is the Perfect example of a Humble Person

In the Magnificat, Our Lady prayed, "My being proclaims the greatness of the Lord, my spirit finds joy in

God my savior, ..." (Luke 1:46-47). Mary recognized that the Incarnation was the gift of God the Father. Our Lady immediately gives God all the praise and glory. For Mary recognized that this gift (The Christ Child) was the cause of her joy...she knew she was gifted and acknowledged the gift and the giver of that gift. But even Mary knew that it was God who saved her. Though sinless from conception (Dogma of Immaculate Conception) Mary was redeemed not at the moment of Baptism as we are, but at the moment of her conception in the womb of her mother, Anna, due to the merits of Jesus Christ.

Humility causes us to acknowledge that despite our gifts we are all sinners.

The importance of Divine Mercy is simply this: it is Jesus who saves everyone including Our Blessed Mother. Humility causes us to seek reconciliation monthly in the Sacrament of Penance as Mary has asked us to do at Medjugorje.

As little children we must always remember that we belong to God, the Father. We are His children and God the Father loves us. Humility allows us to see ourselves as His beloved children.

Self worth is not a remedy devised by psychiatry. Our self worth comes from the fact that we are children of God and temples of the Holy Spirit and God dwells within us.

After delivering a talk on "humility," I returned to my room to go to bed. When I entered my bedroom, the Lord told me to pick up *The Imitation of Christ*. My room is usually in such shambles, I thought to myself, "I'll never find it."

To my amazement, the moment I came into my bedroom, I found this small book by Thomas A. Kempis. I opened it and this is what I read, "Pride and self esteem....the Lord dwelleth in a humble and contrite heart." (i.e. not only one that is humble but one that knows it is a sinner and repents).

I read on. "Hypocrite...the Holy Spirit will flee from the deceitful."

I realized the importance of the insight of the sermon. Humility is a key to the power of the Holy Spirit in the life of an individual as well as a community.

Ralph Martin, in one of his latest books entitled, *The Catholic Church at the End of an Age: What is the Spirit Saying* wrote, "No matter how great the power of evil at work in the world, the power at work in the sons and daughters of God in the Church is greater by far. God will always preserve a remnant bigger than we might expect who will be His own in a special way. The evil and suffering God permits men to do, have as one of their purposes the purification and preparation of a remnant that belongs to Him. God is looking for a meek and humble people who will simply trust in Him." (Zeph 3:12)

Does this remind you of the prayer of Sister Faustina? "Jesus, I trust in you!"

✞✞✞✞✞

Jimmy Lee Jones

Recently, I was asked to say a few words of comfort for a friend who died. His name was Jimmy Lee Jones. He was a black janitor who worked for many years at St. Margaret Mary Parish. He retired about 15 years ago after suffering the effects of heart disease. Jimmy was one of the most humble men I have ever known. I gave this talk at the Pentecost Missionary Baptist Church on April 6, 1996, for a man that truly was "humble of heart."

Today we celebrate the passing of Jimmy Lee Jones, a good, gentle, and humble man. I believe Jimmy is now celebrating in heaven so I decided to wear my red vestments. The gold stole I borrowed from a priest in Gauna, Africa. It was given to him by Pope John Paul II. I figured nothing but the best for my friend Jimmy Lee Jones.

What I would like to share with you was a side of Jimmy that perhaps some of you never saw, even members of his family. The title of this eulogy is "What I learned about being a pastor from Jimmy Lee Jones."

Rule one. When there is more work than 5 people together can do, learn to hide.

You see, after nearly eleven years in the seminary, I was told by the Archbishop that I was too sickly to become a priest. So I was put out of the seminary for nearly a year before I was able to get back. Two years later I was ordained a priest in 1959.

During the time I was out of the seminary, my pastor offered me a job working at St. James Major Church in New Orleans. I thought with a B.A. and M.A. in history, I would surely get a soft job. Instead, Father Schutten put me to work as a janitor.

I was a pretty good janitor, but I never learned to like cutting grass or doing windows.

In 1970, when I was made pastor of St. Margaret Mary, I had a parish without a church. I lived in a trailer for seven years. We had Mass in the cafeteria. There were 12 classrooms and seven trailers, a library and administration building in addition to the cafeteria. All these buildings sat on nearly 15 acres of land, most of which was grass, since Father Tim, the founding pastor, cut down all the trees, except for a few oak trees.

Jimmy Lee Jones drove a school bus, cut 15 acres of grass with an old tractor, took care of the cafeteria and administration building, and did minor repairs. The teachers swept their own classrooms. There was enough work for five men and he was alone.

As soon as Jimmy met me, he said, "Father Tim used to like to cut grass when he wasn't busy." I replied, "Jimmy, I used to be a janitor; I can paint and I preach but I don't like to cut grass and I don't do windows." Well, after I spilled enough cans of paint doing odd jobs, I was told, my job was to get the soft drinks and the beer and leave the paint brush alone.

That first year there was no way Jimmy could do all that was expected of him, so he learned to hide. He could curl up in his bus and only Leola , of fond memory, could ever locate him. So my advice to your pastor is this. If your parishioners want you to do the work of five men, do what I learned from Jimmy Lee Jones... learn to hide.

The second thing I learned from Jimmy Lee Jones was to be humble and have a sense of humor. Jimmy was one of the most humble gifted men I have ever known. One spiritual writer said, "The three rules for the spiritual life is first, humility; second, humility; and third, humility."

But humility without a sense of humor won't get you through life. One summer Jimmy was driving me and the high school youth group to the Smoky Mountains. We started late in the evening and after driving about forty-five minutes our "pretend bus" broke down.

The kids called it a pretend bus because it was 20 years old and always breaking down. Jimmy seemed to be able to fix anything, but this night he was stumped.

"Someone is going to have to leave the bus and hitchhike to the nearest truck stop," I told Jimmy. Jimmy replied, " You probably noticed that I am black. I fix buses, but I don't hitchhike in Mississippi."

So there I was, a big shot priest hitchhiking to the truck stop. We brought back a mechanic with us who worked for fifteen minutes on the bus before he realized that Jimmy had failed to put gas in the bus before we left. So the second rule of being pastor I learned from Jimmy was, "Be humble, but keep your sense of humor."

The third lesson I learned from Jimmy was how to get teenagers to "Be Saved." Every pastor wants his young teens to fall in love with Jesus Christ so that he can be "Lord of their lives." Some pastors do this with great sermons or wonderful programs. Jimmy taught me a shortcut... "Scare them to death."

We got our pretend bus as far as the Smoky Mountains. Our chalet was high in the mountains. This bus didn't seem to have a low gear so it was quite a strain. Finally, as we neared the top of our mountain, we came to a fork in the road. I was sitting in the front seat and Jimmy looked over at me and said, "Do I turn left or right." Now by the time I got the map out to check, the pretend bus had lost its momentum. All of a sudden we began to roll backwards down the mountain. I have never had so many young people commit their lives to Jesus at once. Jimmy recovered quickly. Not only did he save our lives that day, but all of the teens made a quick decision for Jesus. The third rule Jimmy Lee Jones taught me to get teenagers saved was "to scare them to death."

The fourth lesson in Jimmy Lee's life was to learn to suffer in silence. For many years Jimmy endured the pains of heart disease. One of his brothers had died at age 35. I visited him many times in the hospital, but he never complained. I kept paying his health insurance long after he retired at a relatively young age. Jimmy Lee Jones was my friend.

The final lesson I learned from Jimmy was to be a good servant, you needed to be a good friend. I always felt that we were equals. I loved him as a brother.

When Jimmy retired, I had a steak dinner for him at a small house my brother and I own in Diamondhead, Mississippi. He invited his close friends. My secretary and her husband barbecued the steaks and cooked the potatoes. I served as a bartender. I am not sure if drinking alcohol is allowed in this church, but I can assure you that the members of your congregation drank the appropriate drink.

It was just so good to see us white folks serving at tables while Jimmy and his friends basked in the glory. It was a farewell dinner I am sure Jimmy talked about for years.

Conclusion - You need a letter of recommendation

You probably don't realize it but you need a letter of recommendation to get into heaven. Jimmy didn't have any problem getting his letters. But if you're poor, you know it's hard to get a letter of recommendation here on earth.

So Jesus decided to turn the tables on the rich. He decided that before you go to the glory, you need a letter of recommendation. That's why so many rich people don't want to die. They save all their money in IRA's and money markets and stocks and bonds. They do nothing for their sisters and brothers. And they just can't find anyone to write them a decent letter of recommendation.

The poor don't have that problem. I was lucky. I got Jimmy Lee Jones to write me a letter of recommendation to St. Peter before he passed. I would like to read that letter to you. It goes like this.....

Dear St. Peter,

I would like to recommend to you Father Richard L. Carroll. He is a terrible painter. He don't like to cut grass. He don't do windows. But he is my friend...he is my brother.

Love,

Jimmy Lee Jones

---

[1] Pope John Paul, II, *Tertio Millennio Adveniente*, (Boston, MA.: Pauline Books & Media, 1994), page 49, #44.

[2] (Ibid, page 50, #45.)

[3] (Ibid, page 53, #48.)

[4] (Ibid, page 42, #36.)

[5] *Catechism of the Catholic Church*, (New York: Catholic Book Publishing Co., 1992), page 194, #736.

[6] (Pope John Paul, II, *Tertio Millennio Adveniente*, page 10, #4.)

[7] (Ibid, page 49, #43.)

[8] Petrisko, Thomas W., *The Sorrow, The Sacrifice, and the Triumph: The Apparitions, Visions, and Prophecies of Christina Gallagher*, (New York: Simon & Schuster, 1995)

[9] Bright, Bill, *Witnessing without Fear*, (New Life Publications, 1994).

[10] (*Catechism of the Catholic Church*, page 212, #801.)

[11] Fr. Bill McCarthy, MSSA, *Discernment: How do I know if this is of God?*, this information comes from a flyer printed by Fr. McCarthy.

ST. MARGARET MARY

Section Four
Year Three -- God the Father -- 1999

"1999, the third and final year of preparation, will be aimed at broadening the horizons of believers, so that they will see things in the perspective of Christ: in the perspective of the 'Father who is in heaven' (cf. Mt. 5:45), from whom the Lord was sent and to whom he was returned (cf. Jn. 16:28)."[1]
(Pope John Paul, II)

Chapter One
Intercessory Prayer

"Intercession is a prayer of petition which leads us to pray as Jesus did. He is the one intercessor with the Father on behalf of all men, especially sinners. He is 'able for all time to save those who draw near to God through Him, since He always lives to make intercession for them. (Heb. 7:25)' The Holy Spirit 'Himself intercedes for us ... and intercedes for the saints according to the will of God.'(Rom. 8:26-27)"[2]
(Catechism of the Catholic Church)

"Prayer of intercession consists in asking on behalf of another. It knows no boundaries and extends to one's enemies."[3]
(Catechism of the Catholic Church)

"But since Christ is the only way to the Father, in order to highlight His living and saving presence in the Church and the world, the International Eucharistic Congress will take place in Rome, on the occasion of the Great Jubilee. The Year 2000 will be intensely Eucharistic: in the Sacrament of the Eucharist the Savior, who took flesh in Mary's womb twenty centuries ago, continues to offer Himself to humanity as the source of divine life.[4]
(Pope John Paul, II)

✞✞✞✞✞

Jesus is the Way to the Father

Christ is the only way to the Father. The Holy Father in his encyclical *Tertio Millennio Adveniente* tells us that we can reach the Father only by way of Jesus. The path to the Father is through intercessory prayer.

During my stay in the hospital in 1994, I had an unusual experience. As I was praying I realized that I had no relationship to God whom we call Father. I know God the Son through Jesus Christ who is God Incarnate. I love the Holy Spirit because He sanctifies and makes holy. I have seen Him operate in the lives of many of my children. However, I don't know God the Father.

In prayer I asked Jesus the same thing Philip asked Jesus: "'Lord,' Philip said to Him, 'show me the Father and that will be enough for us.' 'Philip,' Jesus replied, 'after I have been with you all this time, you still do not know Me? Whoever has seen Me has seen the Father.'"(John 14:8-9)

Immediately the thought struck me. Philip was lucky he could at least see Jesus who is the Son of the Father. However, what about us, how can we see the Father? At that moment a nurse's aid came in to my room to do some menial task. Again the words of Jesus struck a deep cord. "Whatever you have done for the least, you have done for Me." "The Father and I are one."

God the Father hides behind the least little ones

I began to realize in a very small way that God the Father manifests Himself not through a human presence as God the Son does in Jesus Christ. Nor does God the Father show himself by His power of miracles of grace as God the Holy Spirit does. God the Father almost seems to hide behind the eyes of the least ... His little ones.

You can understand this image a little better if you look at the eyes of your own children. Your small children, boys and girls, are beautiful because of the beauty of their mother. If you look carefully you will recognize that they have their "father's eyes."

In the spiritual order each of you have a "spiritual father." For the Catholic Church that spiritual father is the Pope. By virtue of Baptism, bringing you into eternal life, the priest is your spiritual father. St. Paul was proud to claim his spiritual children as his own. He wrote: "granted you may have ten thousand guardians in Christ, you have only one Father. It was I who begot you in Christ."(1 Corinthians 4:15)

Didn't Jesus Forbid Calling a Priest Father?

In Matthew 23:8-12 Jesus says: "As to you, avoid the title 'Rabbi.' One among you is your teacher, the rest are learners. Do not call anyone on earth your father. Only one is your father, the One in heaven. Avoid being called teachers. Only one is your teachers, the Messiah. The greatest among you will be the one who serves the rest. Whoever exalts himself shall be humbled, but whoever humbles himself shall be exalted."

Was Jesus condemning calling a priest "Father" or your dad "pops"? Was Jesus condemning us for calling a person "teacher" since the word Rabbi means teacher?

Every Protestant Fundamentalist calls their male parent "father". They also call their Sunday school personnel "teachers". We, like St. Paul, understand the context of Jesus condemnation. Jesus was condemning ostentation, not the use of certain words.

All Fatherhood Comes From God

Fatherhood is an act of creation. Parents, in the natural order, beget children; and priests, in the spiritual order, participate in the Fatherhood of God in an extended and limited sense. In the same way, the primary teacher is Jesus Christ. We may participate in an extended sense in

His mission by teaching in the secular sense in school or as parents and religion teachers in the religious sense.

The context and the meaning of words are involved in understanding scripture. Father Roberts, who is a priest from England, gave an example of context affecting our understanding. The first time he visited a friend's home in the United State, the wife was very hospitable and friendly. He felt quite at home. When the friend asked what he thought of his wife, Father Roberts replied, "she is very homely." In England this is a great compliment meaning a good home maker, but to most Americans this means she is rather ugly.

Poem -- My Father's Eyes

A few years ago someone asked if I ever regretted being a priest since it is a lonely life without a wife and children. It is true, it is a lonely life and I certainly would have loved to have children, particularly little girls. The Heavenly Father knew that I could never have supported all the children I would have wanted. So he called me to be a spiritual father to each of you at St. Margaret Mary. He took a little of each of my dreams and implanted them into your hearts.

Jesus made your hearts burn for the love of the Eucharist and a desire to cherish Our Blessed Mother as your own. Our Lord put a thirst in your mouth for evangelism and a talent for singing. He gave you the minds to make money to pay for our church facilities and the hands to work in it. He blessed you with the most beautiful children in the world, and they come in every color and race. And He let them call me father, and best of all, each of you have my eyes.

You also have your Heavenly Father's eyes. After 37 years as a priest, I finally understand a little bit of what

God the Father wants. He wants you to see in my eyes, and the eyes of every priest you meet, a reflection of His love for you. He wants each of you to feel how special you are to your Heavenly Father. Our Heavenly Father hides behind the least of us, because each of you have your Heavenly Father's Eyes.

The Pope is Our Holy Father

In Our Lady's message to Father Gobbi on May 13, 1995, Mary recalls that her first apparition in Fatima took place in the Cova da Iria. Our Lady warns that many of her priest sons are being stricken and becoming tepid. The flock is being scattered and is in danger of eternal perdition.

Our Lady asks that you pray for our Holy Father who is the greatest gift which her Immaculate Heart has given us. He is suffering greatly because he sees humanity so threatened by its own destruction. Mary asks that we pray for our Holy Father whose heart bleeds because of the division in the Church and the errors that are being spread.

Mary tells us that his encyclical letters are beacons of light which shines down from heaven upon the intense darkness which envelops all the world. Our Lady pleads with us to pray for the Pope who is now living the hour of Calvary, of Crucifixion, and his immolation on the altar of his priestly sacrifice.

The final paragraph of that message should be the impetus for all of us wanting to be involved in intercessory prayer. It is through the sacrifice of the Holy Father, Mary tells us, that divine justice will be changed to a great mercy. After the time of trial, which will purify the Earth, there will be a new era foretold and announced by him. In the final times the Pope invites you to cross the bright thresholds of hope.[5]

154

Certainly, every father needs to know that his children have his eyes. Our Heavenly Father knows that each of you have His eyes. You also have the eyes of your spiritual father. For most of us Christians that spiritual father is the Pope, John Paul, II. In our local communities each of you have the eyes of the ones who have brought you into relationship with Jesus Christ in Baptism, your priests, deacons, and ministers in your own Christian faith.

✥✥✥✥

A Call to Intercessory Prayer

The following letter was written to the parishioners at St. Margaret Mary inviting them to a Mass of Inner Healing. The letter brings together many of the facts about Divine Mercy, shame, and inner healing discussed in the course of this book. In this letter I attempted to emphasize the process which led our community to Intercessory Prayer.

The Holy Father tells us that we can only reach God the Father through Jesus. Intercessory Prayer is an integral element of our preparation for the third millennium, which we believe will result in the Triumph of the Immaculate Heart of Mary.

April 1, 1996
Letter to Parishioners

On April 1, 1996 we experienced a Mass of inner healing. Before Mass began we heard the testimony of Lisa and Eric. It was a beautiful story of inner healing brought about by Divine Mercy. After communion we prayed for inner healing and generational healing. Many of our root problems have been passed on to us by our parents or grandparents. After Mass, Father Gallagher and I anointed those who came forward. Father Benson and Father Fisher heard confessions immediately after the healing prayer.

What is "inner healing"? Many of the problems we face, including addictions, can be traced back to our ancestors. Also, many of our root sins result from long hidden guilt or unresolved issues that relate to forgiveness that only Jesus Christ can give us. Many of you have failed to forgive some priest for some long held grudge. The prayers we recite at this Mass address many of these issues asking the Lord Jesus to deal with us through His Divine Mercy.

Confession is an integral part of inner healing for Catholics. As one of the speakers at the Catholic Charismatic Conference in 1996 pointed out, "Deliverance from evil spirits is usually accomplished for Catholics through the Sacrament of Reconciliation." For non-Catholics, who are not privileged to have the Sacrament of Penance, the Holy Spirit usually works directly through gifted healers.

Most of us do not realize the tremendous number of individuals who have been abused in their homes as children either physically, sexually, or verbally. It took an enormous amount of courage for Lisa and Eric to share their story. It is much easier to talk about physical abuse; everyone likes to hear the stories of how my brother, Fr. Ralph, and I were beat with a razor strap. You all figure we deserved it. But there is nothing funny about abuse -- physical, verbal, or sexual.

Lisa and Eric's story is not about "shame". It is about Divine Mercy. Jesus has already taken the shame that most of us carry on His own shoulders when He hung on the cross.

Divine Mercy allows us as individuals to see ourselves as God sees us. This includes the root causes of our problems hidden because of shame. Once brought to the light, Jesus can heal us. On Good Friday, we will begin the Novena of Divine Mercy, given by Sister Faustina. It will culminate with Mass at 3:00 p.m. on Sunday, April 13, 1996.

My beloved children, I asked that you pray a simple pray every night. It comes from last Sunday's Gospel of St. John, "Heavenly Father, we are blind, let us see ourselves as You see us." This was the prayer that I prayed for myself that resulted in the incredible miracle of Divine Mercy for me in March 1994. It was a life changing event. As a result of that religious experience, 1200 adults out of the 2500 adults who attend Mass on Sunday at St. Margaret Mary went to confession on Tuesday, March 15, 1994. Many of us believe that St. Margaret Mary will be a center for Divine Mercy in our area.

✜✜✜✜✜

Our Lady at Garabandal 1961- 1965

At Garabandal in 1961, Our Lady predicted what Sister Faustina, the Polish nun given the responsibility to spread Divine Mercy, was told years earlier that every human being would experience an illumination . They would see themselves as God sees them. The experience of Eric and Lisa was that illumination; they shared their story so you can prepare for this miracle in your life. When you experience what is called by some "a mini-judgment," it may well be a very frightening experience. For those of you who are prepared it will be an incredible experience of Divine Mercy.

Certain things stand out at Garabandal. In an article entitled "The Warning and Miracle: Interview with the seers," the visionaries at Garabandal discussed the warning, the great miracle and the possibility of the punishment.

1.   **The warning** - Everyone will be given the grace to see themselves as they are. One of the visionaries at Garabandal, Conchita said, "the warning is like a purification for the miracle. ... the warning will be a correction of the conscience of the world. For those who do not know Christ [non-Christian] they will believe it is a warning from God."

Conchita went on to explain: "The most important thing about that day is that   everyone in the whole world will see a sign,   a grace, or a punishment within themselves - in other words, a warning. They will find themselves all alone in the world no matter where they are at the time, alone with their conscience right before God. They will then see all their sins and what their sins have caused."

Conchita concluded by saying: "What I remember now is that the Virgin told me that before the miracle God will be sending us a warning so as to purify us or prepare us to see the miracle and in this way we may draw enough grace to change our lives toward God."[6]

2.   **The great miracle** - at Garabandal, we are told that following the "mini judgment," there will be a great miracle. It will be able to be seen and photographed.

Joey Lomangino, the great apostle of Garabandal, was told by Mari Loli that the warning and the great miracle will occur in the same year. Joey, blind since he was sixteen, visited Padre Pio over 30 years ago. Padre Pio indicated to Joey that he should go to Garabandal. Apparently, Padre Pio was gifted with a vision of the great miracle before his death. Although these apparitions at Garabandal have never been approved by the Church, the insight of this deceased Friar lend credence to the words of these visionaries.

Fr. Bernardino Cennamo, OFM attested to Padre Pio's belief in Garabandal. In a letter dated July 4, 1969, to Mr. Anthony O'Brien of London England, Fr. Cennamo wrote:

> "... I was in Garabandal May 30 of this year [1969] and I saw Conchita (again). The same Padre Pio during his lifetime had guaranteed the authenticity of the apparitions of the Virgin. He met Conchita in San Giovanni Rotondo [1966] and furthermore, during the last days of his life, he spoke with his brothers, leaving a personal message for the principal protagonist of the apparitions. The message, entrusted to Padre Pellegrino, was ... given to Conchita at Lourdes in October of the past year, I too being present ..."

"Conchita received her first letter from Padre Pio on March 3, 1962, and answered him the same day, her letter containing a personal message from Our Lady." Conchita told Padre Pio he would see the miracle before his death. Fr. Cennamo later indicated that Padre Pio did see the miracle.[7]

"Fr. Cennamo said to Conchita that he did not believe in the apparitions until Padre Pio told him to give her the veil that would cover his face after his death. ... He saw the Miracle before he died. He told me so himself."[8]

In the article "The Warning and the Miracle: Interview with the Seers," Conchita was asked about the great miracle. She responded: "I will tell you all that I can just as the Virgin told it to me. She told me that God was going to perform a great miracle and that there would be no doubt about the fact that it was a miracle. It will come directly from God with no human intervention. A day will come - and she told me the day the month and the year so I know the exact date."

When asked the day, Conchita replied, "it is coming soon but I can't reveal it until eight days before the date."

Conchita went on to explain that the extraordinary sign would remain until the end of time and that "... everyone will be able to see and touch but not feel." Our Lady promised that Joey Lamangino would be cured of his blindness on that day. Conchita was also told that the miracle would occur between March and May.[9]

Through the warning, all will know the power of God. The purpose of the miracle therefore, is to convert the whole world so that souls may be saved and peace exist. If the world does not repent, then the chastisement will befall mankind.

After the miracle, a permanent, visible, supernatural, "sign" will remain at the pines in Garabandal until the end of time.

3.   **The punishment** (chastisement) - the children of Garabandal were told that if world does not convert after the miracle, a great punishment would ensue.

I am sure that some readers will question the extensive use of an apparition site that has not been approved by the Church after thirty years. My personal devotion to Padre Pio, and my conviction that he will be canonized by the Holy Father convinces me that there is much to be learned from Garabandal.

First, the danger to the world if conversion does not follow the warning and the manifestation of the great miracle. The *Book of Revelation* gives ample proof that the times of tribulation will be devastating. Anything we can do to convince the world to convert to Jesus Christ will lessen or diminish the chances for catastrophes.

Secondly, the fact that the great miracle will be Eucharistic should bolster our enthusiasm and hope. Our Holy Father, Pope John Paul, II points to the third millennium as Eucharistic. If faith in the real presence of Jesus Christ results, conversions will abound.

At Fatima in 1917, Our Lady indicated that there would be a triumph of the Immaculate Heart of Mary and an era of peace. The peace will become a reality when belief in the Real Presence in the Eucharist is proclaimed worldwide. The Triumph of Our lady will be one of intercession. Only the Holy Spirit can bring about a deep rooted belief in Jesus Christ present in Holy Communion.

The Final Warning! Are we ready?

One of the most startling messages given to Fr. Gobbi by Our Lady occurred at the Shrine of Our Lady of Guadeloupe, in Mexico City, December 1994. Our Lady told Father Gobbi, "I confirm to you, that by the jubilee year 2000, there will take place the Triumph of my Immaculate Heart."

In numerous locations around the world, Our Lady is saying the same thing, "my children are not prepared!"

What did Our Blessed Mother mean that her children are not prepared? Certainly, there are very few individuals who are prepared to experience the "mini-judgment" or "illumination" predicted at Garabandal and revealed to Fr. Gobbi. Sister Faustina speaks of the same type of religious experience of Divine Mercy which you have heard of in my own testimony as well as that of Lisa and Eric.

Our Blessed Mother told Fr. Gobbi "...that tongues of fire from the Holy Spirit would come down upon all her poor children. You will see your own selves in the mirror of the truth and the holiness of God. It will be like a **judgment in miniature** which will open the door of your heart to receive the great gift of Divine Mercy."[10]

At. St. Margaret Mary we have been led to prepare for this "mini judgment" or "illumination" through the Sacrament of Penance.

Our First stage of preparation was repentance. As a result of listening to Our Lady, 1200 adults came to confession on March 15, 1994. Our Holy Father in the encyclical *Tertio Millennio Adveniente* tells us that **repentance** is a key element of our preparation for the third millennium. It will also prepare you for the Triumph of Our Lady should this occur soon. The Sacrament of Penance must be revived in every Catholic parish.

Second Stage of Preparation

Our second stage of preparation at St. Margaret Mary has been discipleship. We have committed our resources to making Jesus the Lord of our lives. This has changed the focus of our parish from the simple instruction of children in parochial school and CCD to adult catechesis.

In order to make Jesus the Lord of our lives we must know him in order to love him. Hence the program to prepare adults to become "fully armed disciples of Jesus Christ," involves scripture, theology, spiritual direction and prayer.

Scripture tells us: "... no one can say: 'Jesus is Lord,' except in the Holy Spirit."(1 Corinthians 12:3) Life in the Spirit Retreats are a key element in this process. Catholics must learn to be "born again."

Our retreat team, composed of priests, teens, and young adults has developed into a tremendous form of peer ministry. In 1996 we plan to utilize this group, not only to give retreats and days of recollection, but to serve as discussion leaders in the Confirmation program for our High School Sophomores.

Intercessory Prayer - The Third Stage

I believe that Our Blessed Mother will use this community in a powerful way to be evangelists of Divine Mercy through intercessory prayer. This is the third stage of preparing for the Triumph of Our Lady.

I was privileged to hear Fr. Matthew Naikomphrambil who is called the Billy Graham of India. He has preached to crowds that number in the hundreds of thousands. But in speaking to the priests and lay leaders in 1996 in New Orleans, he told a story that illustrated how Our Mother Mary will use us through intercessory prayer.

Fr. Matthew began a prayer meeting on Thursday nights in India and fourteen people came. By the third week, he had only twenty, one of whom was an insane woman. Fr. Matthew prayed over her for fifteen minutes and nothing happened. Finally, he left the group and went to pray in the chapel quietly.

In the chapel, Jesus spoke to his heart "Change the time and format of the prayer meeting. Meet on Saturday from 9:00 a.m. to 3:00 p.m. . Half of the time should be spent in praise and worship, the other half praying for the evangelization of the world. Will you do this?" Without any hesitation Fr. Matthew said, "Yes". When Fr. Matthew returned to the group the woman was healed. He began the Saturday Intercessory Prayer Group. Within two years, it has grown from the original fourteen to ten to twelve thousand each week.

As I heard Fr. Matthew's story I knew how we are to prepare for Divine Mercy ....We are to become a people of intercessory prayer. For four years now, our school children have been doing this every day. Now it is our turn.

Frankly, I didn't know the best time. For most of us Friday night is the ideal time. I asked my class that is involved in evangelization training if they would be willing to meet either on Saturday morning or on Friday nights. They were enthusiastic and said they will do either.

I met with the core group of our Charismatic Prayer Group and I gave them the option. If you want to continue the prayer group as it is on Friday nights, I will be happy to begin our intercessory prayer on Saturday morning. I left it up to them.

I explained that I have been invited to speak at a national convention in Philadelphia. They are attempting to bring together Charismatics, the Marian Movement, the Cursillo, Marriage Encounter, Magnificat and any other Catholic group to see what the Holy Spirit is calling us.

As I spoke to our own charismatic leaders they decided unless it was unanimous, they would continue on Friday night. I shared with them the image of the "yeast in the dough". I believe the Holy Spirit put His Spirit in all of these Catholic groups I mentioned above. He wanted them all to work together to bring about the bread of life throughout the world. But every gifted group decided they didn't want to be part of the whole. They each wanted to be the whole loaf. The result has been a calamity for the church. Today every group is suffering the malaise. Numbers have fallen and our churches are empty.

Would our Charismatics be willing to surrender their individuality for the good of the church? Would the other Spirit filled groups respond to the call of the Holy Spirit to join together as one people of praise? It would mean a totally revamped form of prayer for all of us. But I promised at least one priest would be present for the entire meeting.

Frankly, I was amazed that after a brief period of discernment the leaders came to the rectory to tell me, they would listen to Our Lady, that they would "Do whatever Jesus told them to do". We will begin the Friday after "Mercy Sunday", i.e. April 18, 1996.

Our Lady's Crusade

You have been called individually by name by Our Blessed Mother to join her crusade of prayer. The Divine Mercy of her Son will be the   saving grace for countless souls if each of our Spirit filled groups join together including our youth. Will you become an evangelizer for Mary through intercessory prayer. If you do, every Catholic parish will be used by her for the conversion of the United States. Can our group leaders from the various groups and ministries put aside their own prideful dreams and do what Mary wants? Will you be her evangelizers of Divine Mercy through intercessor prayer. The first general meeting took place on Friday, April 18, beginning at 7:00 p.m.

If you say, "Yes" to Our Lady, you will be part of the triumph of The Immaculate Heart of Mary which was predicted by her at Fatima in 1917. When you children or grandchildren ask you in five years time how world peace was achieved. Tell them what you did! You became a slave of Jesus through Mary; you helped bring about the triumph of the Immaculate Heart of Mary. The era of peace that they will enjoy was brought about because you listened to Mary when she said, "Whatever Jesus tells you to do....do it".

✝ ✝ ✝ ✝ ✝

Intercessory Prayer -- A Crusade of Prayer

I feel that Our Blessed Mother has asked her Son Jesus for a special grace to fall on St. Margaret Mary Parish. This is the grace that this community be one of the parishes used by the Holy Spirit to help bring about the Triumph of the Immaculate Heart of Mary, predicted by Our Lady at Fatima in 1917.

This call will resound in the hearts of her children who have worked tirelessly for the building up of the Mystical Body of Jesus Christ. Unfortunately, you are now but a remnant!

In her name I would like to issue what I believe is her final call - to prepare for the Triumph of the Immaculate Heart of Mary through Divine Mercy.

It was only after hearing Fr. Matthew Naikomphrambil, a priest from India, at a recent charismatic conference in New Orleans (April, 1996), that I realized the final piece of the Holy Spirit's plan was now to be put into effect - healing and Divine Mercy through intercessory prayer.

Very much like the freshman algebra student who looked in the back of the book and found the answer to the question, I thought, "What is there left for the Remnant Church to do to prepare for the third millennium and the Triumph of the Immaculate Heart of Mary predicted by Mary in 1917?"

The answer was given - intercessory prayer. But like the young algebra student I asked the Lord Jesus, "How do we get from the question to the answer?" And Jesus said: "trust in Me!" In the end, Sister Faustina was right. All of us must say, "Jesus, I trust in You!"

Like fools for Jesus Christ we decided as a parish to become like little children with the firm conviction that the Holy Spirit would teach us the power of intercessory prayer.

The time of prayer would be critical. All of you have busy lives, filled with time-consuming tasks. The Friday night charismatic prayer group leaders were asked if they would allow us the opportunity to become a people of intercessory prayer. The charismatic pastoral team decided to do: "whatever Jesus tells us to do." They sacrificed their own egos so they could teach others the importance of humility and the necessity of being part of the Triumph of the Immaculate Heart of Mary.

On Thursday, April 18, I invited the leaders for all 65 ministries of St. Margaret Mary to a meeting. This included the leadership of all choirs including the Friday night choir and all members of the prayer teams, trained by Fr. Benson and Sister Veronica and commissioned by me in December, 1995. Nearly 75 adults showed up at this meeting. Our first intercessory prayer meeting was held Friday, April 19, 1996.

Each participant was given a list of the large core group of intercessory prayer. This was to ensure our goal of a parish wide intercessory prayer group. Each ministry was represented.

Being a pastor I have no right to stifle the Holy Spirit. At the same time, I expect the gifts of the Holy Spirit will be under the authority of the pastor. It was agreed that the gifts of the Holy Spirit would be allowed to flourish, but no one would be permitted to pass judgment on anyone. Humility and love will be the hallmark of The Remnant Church. No matter how great a gift you have from the Holy Spirit, if it is not under the authority of the pastor, it will be a force for division in our parish.

A small core group of prayer partners were selected. Two different individuals had given "words of knowledge," to pray for and with our priests. "Surround yourselves with powerful prayer partners during this time of battle." The small group functions in this fashion. They meet with the priests an hour before the Friday night meeting to pray for our priests and to discern the direction of the intercessory prayer meeting. During the Friday meeting they will be used as a group to discern words of knowledge or scripture and be responsible for sharing these with the community.

The Apparitions of Jesus to St. Margaret Mary

St. Margaret Mary Alacoque' is an appropriate model to our community of intercessory prayer. This patroness of our parish, had four apparitions of Our Lord, Jesus Christ while she was at prayer.

"The first apparition took place on the Feast of St. John the Evangelist, that is, December 27th, probably in 1673." St. Margaret Mary relates it as follows:
"One day, being before the Blessed Sacrament, as I had some leisure time, I was so overwhelmed by this Divine

presence as to forget myself and the place where I was. I abandoned myself to this Divine Spirit, surrendering my heart to the might of His love. ... He disclosed to me the marvels of His love and the unutterable secrets of His Sacred Heart, which He had always concealed from me, until He opened it to me now for the first time...

"He said to me: 'My Divine Heart is so passionately inflamed with love for men, and for you in particular, that, not being able any longer to contain within Itself the flames of Its ardent charity, it must needs spread them abroad through your means, and manifest itself to men, that they may be enriched with its precious treasures which I unfold to you, and which contain the sanctifying and salutary graces that are necessary to hold them back from the abyss of ruin. **And I have chosen you, an abyss of unworthiness and ignorance, for the accomplishment of this great design, that all this may be My work.'** ... Hitherto you have taken but the name of My slave; I give you now the title of the beloved disciple of My Sacred Heart."[11]

It is of great significance to our community at St. Margaret Mary that the Mass of Inner Healing and Healing of Ancestry takes place on the first Friday of the month. Devotion to the Sacred Heart of Jesus, which includes attending Mass for nine consecutive first Fridays. The following are the promises Jesus gave to those who comply with His requests.

Promises of the Sacred Heart of Jesus to
Saint Margaret Mary Alacoque'

1. I will give them all the graces necessary for their state of life.
2. I will establish peace in their families.
3. I will bless every house in which the picture of My Heart shall be exposed and honored.

4.   I will console them in all their difficulties.
5.   I will be their refuge during life and especially at the hour of death.
6.   I will shed abundant blessings upon all their undertakings.
7.   Sinners shall find in My Heart a fountain and boundless ocean of mercy.
8.   Tepid souls shall become fervent.
9.   Fervent souls shall rise speedily to great perfection.
10.   I will give to priests the power of touching the hardest hearts.
11.   Those who propagate this devotion shall have their names written in My Heart never to be blotted out.
12.   I promise thee, in the excessive mercy of My Heart, that My all-powerful love will grant to all who communicate on the first Friday of the month for nine consecutive months, the grace of final penitence; they shall not die in My displeasure nor without their sacrament; My Divine Heart shall be their safe refuge in this last moment.

✠✠✠✠✠

One of the things many have asked for is more time for confession. It was decided that a priest would be available every Friday during the praise and worship time for confession. It is important that we allow those whose hearts are softened by Divine Mercy to have the first opportunity for reconciliation. Most have already met the conditions laid down by the Sacred Heart of Jesus for the 9 First Fridays. We must be responsive to the deep spiritual needs of those who will return to the faith through intercessory prayer.

Many have asked for more opportunities for Masses of inner healing. Consequently, every First Friday, we will have a Mass of inner healing followed by anointing by the priests and prayer team members.

We all pray for the day that our intercessory prayer will be powerful enough to result in miraculous physical healings. However first Our Lady must teach us to heal our own broken hearts since so many of us have been injured or affected by our families.

One member of the small core group shared a word. "Mary said, 'I brought forth the physical body of Jesus, you must bring forth the spiritual body of Jesus Christ. I have done my part. Now you must do yours.'"

May 3, 1996 was the First Friday, our intercessory prayer meeting began with the rosary at 7 p.m. followed by praise and worship music. All the choirs were asked to sit in the choir area. At 8 p.m., we began the Mass of Inner Healing and intergenerational Healing.

Intercessory Prayer for the Whole Church

A component of intercessory prayer would be testimonials of how the Holy Spirit was changed your life by working in this ministry to which you have been called. Each week we have one testimonial which recognizes how the Holy Spirit was working in each ministry. We will also encourage testimonials on "healing."

Fr. Matthew mentioned at the Charismatic Conference that their prayer meeting involved both praise and worship music and intercessory prayer for the **evangelization of the entire church**. I felt that it was significant that we pray for the conversion of the world for Jesus Christ. Although it is important to pray for our personal needs, these are secondary to the evangelization of the world. It is the desire of God the Father that the Church be One.

The first intercessory prayer group met on Friday, April 19, 1996, with 150 in attendance. The format for intercessory prayer was discussed and approved by the small core group. Everyone was in agreement that the format would be altered as the Holy Spirit leads us.

Format for Friday Night Prayer Meeting

7:00 p.m. Rosary recited as participants begin to assemble

7:30   Leaders open with prayer to the Holy Spirit.

7:30-8:00 Praise and Worship Songs

8:00   1st Week - Message of the month - Our Lady of
                Medjugorje
                     Song to follow or silence
           2nd Week - Fr. Gobbi speaks to his beloved
                priests
                     Song to follow or silence
           3rd Week - Apostolate of Holy Motherhood
                     Song to follow or silence
           4th Week - Diary of Sister Faustina
                     Song to follow or silence
           Weekly - Leader reads the Act of Consecration
                to Sacred and Merciful Heart of Jesus - Fr.
                Kosicki

8:15   Intercessory Prayer for World Evangelization (taken
           from Good Friday liturgy)
           1.   For the Church_____
           2.   For the Pope_____
           3.   For the Clergy and Laity_____
           4.   For those preparing for Baptism_____
           5.   For the Unity of Christians_____
           6.   For the Jewish People_____
           7.   For those who do not believe in Christ_____
           8.   For those who do not believe in God_____

9.   For all in Public Office_____
10.   For those in Special Need_____

8:45   10 Minute Testimonies - "How the Holy Spirit
       Changed my Life"

9:00   Mass - Includes instruction by priest or deacon.

10:00 Meeting ends - Prayer teams will pray over those
       who wish.

Confessions - 7:30 - 8:30 p.m.

First Friday Meetings -- A Mass of Inner Healing

Once a month on the first Friday, we have a mass of inner healing which begins at 8:00 p.m. using Fr. Al Fredette's material. These inner healing masses have been a great success in the past and may bring a large number of the community into intercessory prayer.

A member of the Catholic Charismatic Renewal of New Orleans had sent a copy of a booklet of a workshop by Fr. Kosicki to Fr. Benson last November. The booklet was entitled *A workshop on interceding as a priestly people: Living Eucharistically*, dated Sept. 20 & 21, 1995. I would certainly recommend Fr. Kosicki's book published by Divine Mercy International entitled *Interceding as a Priestly People: Living Eucharistically*. It includes the Act of Consecration to the Sacred and Merciful Heart of Jesus.

✠ ✠ ✠ ✠ ✠

First Friday
May 5, 1996

The first Friday Mass of Inner Healing on May 5, 1996, was a huge success. Approximately 450 people attended. A highlight of the service was the testimony of Mrs. Kathleen Keefe, founding and director of Peace Through Divine Mercy Apostolate from Yonkers, N. Y.

After Mass there were three prayer teams that anointed those who came forward. In the final chapter, I will share the story of one woman who was healed of her shame at that service. I believe her account will impress upon you how forgiveness, release of shame and miracles are so closely tied together.

Many priests have been turned off by witnessing "healing services." We have seen gifted priests and laymen claiming a healing of some minor ailment, like a headache or backache that could be relieved by an aspirin. At the same time we have seen people in wheelchairs prayed over and remain untouched.

Every priest understands the great value of suffering. St. Paul put it best when he wrote: "... I fill up what is lacking in the sufferings of Christ for the sake of his body, the Church." (Colossians 1:24) St. Paul didn't mean Jesus didn't suffer enough. Rather he was showing us by his own example that God the Father allows us to enter into the mystery of redemption by our own suffering.

Nevertheless, there is much we as Catholics need to learn about healing if we are to be used by the Holy Spirit. There is no doubt in my mind that the healing of shame which we are beginning to see is an incredible miracle. Most priests have also witnessed in their own ministry how

Jesus has used the Sacrament of the Anointing of the Sick, to heal in a marvelous way.

It is certainly true that **deliverance** from evil spirits most often occurs for Catholics in the confessional. The Sacrament of Penance is a powerful tool for dealing with the demonic.

However, we can learn much from our Protestant brothers and sisters who are involved in the healing ministry. Far too often we fail to be open to the power of the Holy Spirit and become muted instruments of Divine Mercy. We need to pray with an expectant faith, knowing that God the Father does want to heal us our shame. Jesus took that shame on the cross at Calvery

Picture of Sorrowful Mother

Recently I received a donation of a painting of the sorrowful mother from a Presbyterian couple, Dr. and Mrs. Richard Dickie. In this framed canvas, which measures 6' X 4', Our Lady is seen holding her son who had just been taken down from the cross. I put the picture in our Blessed Sacrament Chapel with the hope that if "intercessory prayer" is truly part of the Holy Spirit's plan for Our Lady's triumph, she would, as a good mother, get the Holy Spirit to teach us how to pray as Our Heavenly Father wants us to do.

The Illumination or Mini-Judgment

For weeks now I have tried to get my parishioners, to pray to Our Heavenly Father "let me see myself as You see me." This is the gift that Lisa and Eric shared at the last healing mass. It was the same gift that I experienced two years ago.

Will this illumination result in unity within the church? I believe it will if the Holy Spirit agrees to build a few models of parish unity throughout the world. That is where I see the role of the remnant church to model unity within the church.

I believe the Holy Father, in his encyclical Tertio Millennio Adveniente, lays out a blue print for unity as he prepares us for the jubilee year 2000. Hopefully, this will fulfill the promise of Our Lady at Fatima in 1917 that her Immaculate Heart would triumph over Satan and world peace would occur. Mary has told Fr. Gobbi that this triumph will occur by the year 2000. What a glorious day it will be if we are part of her plan to bring out the final defeat of Satan and a world where the will of God the Father is done, "as it is in heaven."

Chapter Two
"Ut Unum Sint" - That They May Be One

*"Perhaps the most convincing form of ecumenism is the
ecumenism of the saints and of the martyrs. The communio
sanctorum speaks louder than the things which divide
us."[12]*
(Pope John Paul, II)

*"O Father most Holy protect them with Your Name which
You have given me [that they may be one even as We are
one]. ... I gave them Your word, and the world has hated
them for it; they do not belong to the world [any more than
I belong to the world]. ... Consecrate them by means of
truth."*
(John 17:11-17)

*"I do not pray for them alone. I pray also for those who
will believe in me through their word, that all may be one
as You, Father, are in me, and I in You; I pray that they
may be [one] in Us, that the world may believe that You
sent Me."*
(John 17:20-21)

✝✝✝✝✝

It is quite clear that the vision Pope John Paul, II has
of the third millennium is that of unity. One worldwide
church is the burning desire of the present pope.

As we can see in John 17:20, union (i.e. "that we
may all be one") is a fervent prayer of Jesus Christ shortly
before He began His passion and death. Jesus' desire for
union seems to be the consuming desire of the Messiah.

Since we know that Jesus came "to do the will of
His heavenly Father," unity must also be a primary goal of

God the Father. Reunion, therefore, among Christian churches must be a dream that all Christians embrace.

In his encyclical "Ut Unum Sint" Pope John Paul, II prays for Christian "communion." The word communion is surprising since you would expect "union" or "unity" or "reunion." The Holy Father apologizes for the scandal of divided churches. He invites separated churches to join him in the years before 2000 by renewing hope and trust in Christ's words: "I pray that they may be [one] in Us."

✞✞✞✞✞

God the Father's Plan

Pope John Paul, II tells us it is God's plan that all the churches and the Bishop of Rome, in particular, work to gather all Christians into unity. "... the Church," he says, "... is sent to the world to announce and witness, to make present and spread the mystery of communion which is essential to her, and gather all people and things into Christ, so as to be for all an 'inseparable sacrament of unity.'"[13]

In an excellent article entitled "Can the Papacy Change" the authors Robert Monyhan and Antoneo Gaspari (*Inside the Vatican* June-July 1995) make an important point. Thirty years have now passed since the second Vatican Council. "Full canonical reunion now seems a remote prospect, perhaps even impossible in this world."[14] However, the Holy Father clearly believes that some type of "communion" in keeping with the prayer for Jesus seems possible. Pope John Paul, II certainly wants to make the effort to bring about this during his pontificate. Communion with other Christian churches is the Holy Father's goal for the third millennium.

Pope John Paul, II, in his encyclical on unity, sees himself as a direct heir of Vatican II thinking. The Holy Father embraces and develops the conciliar commitments and aspirations. The only possible development now seems along the line of "communion. He embraces this thinking.

Re-Interpreting Vatican II

In his encyclical "Ut Unum Sint" the Holy Father writes: "On the eve of His sacrifice on the Cross, Jesus Himself prayed to the Father for His disciples and for all those who believe in Him, that they *might be one*, a living communion"[15]

The Holy Father continues: "The faithful are *one* because, in the Spirit, they are in *communion* with the Son and, in Him, share in His *communion* with the Father. .... For the Catholic Church, then, the *communion* of Christians is none other than the manifestation in them of the grace by which God makes them sharers in his own *communion*, which is his eternal life. Christ words 'that they may be one' are thus His prayer to the father, that the **Father's plan** may be accomplished..."[16]

The Holy Father summarizes his argument: "to believe in Christ means to desire unity; to desire unity means to desire the Church; to desire the Church means to desire the communion of grace which corresponds to the Father's plan for all eternity. Such is the meaning of Christ's prayer."[17]

Division Within the Body of Christ

There are profound divisions within the Catholic Church. These divisions need to be overcome. We are not a conservative or a liberal Catholic Church. We are One Holy, Catholic, and Apostolic.

Despite the decision of the Anglican Church to ordain women, the Holy Father has not given up hope. Pope John Paul, II says: "people of both sides were to blame." When you read this encyclical on unity it makes you wonder ... if only he had been Pope during the beginning of the reformation. Our division might never have happened.

The Holy Father writes: "the elements of sanctification and truth present in the other Christian communities, in a degree which varies from one to the other constitute the objective basis of communion, albeit imperfect, which exists between them and the Catholic Church."[18]

The Holy Father continues: "'the elements of sanctification and truth' which in various ways are present and operative beyond the visible boundaries of the Catholic Church: 'For there are many who honor Sacred Scripture, taking it as a norm of belief and of action, and who show a true religious zeal. They lovingly believe in God the Father Almighty and in Christ, Son of God and Savior. They are consecrated by Baptism, through which they are united with Christ. They also recognize and receive other sacraments within their own churches or eccesial communities. Many of them rejoice in the episcopate, celebrate the Holy Eucharist, and cultivate devotion toward the Virgin Mother of God ...'" Citing the decree on ecumenism from Vatican II, the Pope writes: "All those justified by faith through Baptism are incorporated into Christ. They, therefore, have a right to be honored by the title of Christian and are properly regarded as brothers and sisters in the Lord by the sons and daughters of the Catholic Church."[19]

In the Heart of the encyclical the Holy Father points to the primacy of prayer. At St. Margaret Mary this is key to the importance of intercessory prayer; not merely praying for our own personal needs, but rather having a universal focus on the power of prayer we must pray for the entire church splintered by our own sins as well as those outside the church. The Pope writes: "When brothers and sisters who are not in perfect communion with one another come together to pray, the Second Vatican Council defines the prayers *as the soul of the whole ecumenical movement.*"[20] "When Christians pray together, the goal of unity seems closer. ... If Christians, despite their divisions, can grow ever more united in common prayer around Christ, they will grow in the awareness of how little divides them in comparison to what unites them."[21]

Reunion with Orthodox

Doctrinal differences between the orthodox church and the Holy See at Rome are minor. The major problem is the Petrine office - the papacy. The orthodox feel communion with Rome would involve submission to Rome which they feel historically and canonically unjustified.

In *Ut Unum Sint* Pope John Paul, II tries to surmount this problem. He emphasized both oriental and western tradition without requiring that one be subservient to the other. In paragraph 95, Pope John Paul, II writes: "As Bishop of Rome I am fully aware ... that Christ ardently desires the full and visible communion of all these communities in which, by virtue of God's faithfulness, His spirit dwells. I am convinced I have a particular responsibility in this regard, above all in acknowledging the ecumenical aspirations of the majority of the Christian communities and in heeding the request made of me to find a way of exercising the primacy which, while in no way renouncing what is essential to its mission, is nevertheless open to a new situation."[22]

Dilemma -- Can Change Take Place?

The Holy Father describes the See of Peter as a seat of mercy which leads to peace, the place of a watchkeeper and the servant of unity. Given the imperfect union due to the rejection of primacy and difference in dogma, can any real change take place? The Holy Father makes it clear that full and visible communion with Rome, means acceptance of primacy and dogma. Pope John Paul, II quotes his words to the Patriarch of Constantinople: "I ... pray the Holy Spirit to shine His light upon us, enlightening all the Pastors and theologians of our Churches, that we may seek - together, of course - the form in which this ministry may accomplish a service of love recognized by all concerned."[23]

The Holy Spirit Alone

Just as he does in the encyclical *Tertio Millennio Adveniente* so also in *Ut Unum Sint*, the Holy Father calls upon the Holy Spirit to effect that unity.

How can the Church become one. His answer: "through *hope* in the Spirit, Who can banish from us the painful memories of our separation ... with God nothing is impossible."[24]

Martyrdom -- A Sign of Unity

The Holy Father sees martyrdom of Catholics and Protestants as the sign that might bring the Church together as one. The Pope writes: "perhaps the most convincing form of ecumenism is the ecumenism of the saints and martyrs. The *communio sanctorum* speaks louder than the things which divide us."[25]

The Holy Father points out in the same encyclical: "At the end of the second millennium, the Church has once again become a Church of martyrs."[26] What is significant is that these martyrs are not only Catholic but orthodox, Anglicans, and Protestants as well.

Pope John Paul, II recognizes that each martyr has been a witness to Christ by the shedding of blood. As we honor the martyrs in other faiths we recognize our mutual bond to Jesus Christ and to his Church.

The vision at our priest retreat in San Giovanni in 1995 showed that the "blood of the clergy will cover St. Peter's Basilica." Fr. Jozo, the first pastor in Medjugorje at the time that the apparitions of Our Lady began in Yugoslavia, predicted persecution for the clergy in our own country. We can expect martyrdom as the price to be paid for Christian unity.

The Role of the Holy Spirit

It is God the Father's plan to bring about union in the Church. According to Pope John Paul, II this union can come about only by the power of the Holy Spirit. The role of Mary is that of intercessor. Like Queen Esther she pleads for the survival of the people of God.

Intercessory prayer is the joining of our voices together with Our Lady to plead for the conversion of the world. Our prayer is that of Jesus Christ Himself, the "One mediator between God and man." The prayer of Jesus is clear: "Father, the hour has come! Give glory to Your Son that Your Son may give glory to You..."(John 17:1) Jesus goes on to say: "O Father most holy, protect them with Your name which You have given Me [that they may be one, even as We are one]."(John 17:11) "I do not pray for them alone. I pray also for those who will believe in Me through their word, that all may be one as You, Father, are in Me, and I in You; I pray that they may be [one] in Us, that the world may believe that You sent Me."(John 17:20-21)

Chapter Three
Obstacles to the Father's Plan

Obstacle One
St. John Bosco's Vision

On the back of my book, *The Remnant Church*, I put a picture of the Pope of the end times steering the church through troubled waters. According to St. John Bosco, the Holy Father steers the Barque of Peter, guided by two pillars of light. One column is the Eucharist, the other column of light is Our Blessed Mother, Mary.

In St. Margaret Mary this image was very helpful in developing the idea of a remnant church. We devoted great effort in deepening the faith of our parishioners in the Eucharist. Perpetual Adoration began at St. Margaret Mary in December 1983. The love of the Eucharist has deepened as people spent more time in prayer before the Blessed Sacrament.

The other pillar of light is Our Blessed Mother. At St. Margaret Mary we have encouraged love for Mary in many different ways. First Saturday devotions, recitation of the rosary after daily mass, total consecration to Jesus through Mary according to St. Louis de Montforte, daily consecration to the Immaculate Heart of Mary are a few of the ways we have encouraged devotion to Our Lady.

For four years, our school children have had a prayer Cenacle for each class where they pray the rosary, praise God through song and learn intercessory prayer with the help of fifty prayer moms. This is a weekly Cenacle similar to what Fr. Gobbi suggested.

We have encouraged a love for our Holy Father, Pope John Paul, II. We proudly hung a portrait of the

Pope in the vestibule of our church. Pope John Paul, II is a hero to most of us at St. Margaret Mary.

The Rest of the Story
The Martydom of the Pope

There is more to the visions of St. John Bosco. John Bosco saw the pope of the end times wounded and recover. However, the pope is wounded a second time and dies. His successor is elected very quickly.

The martydom of Pope John Paul, II could precipitate a crisis in the Catholic Church. His death could unleash the forces of Satan and result in the tribulation found in the *Book of Revelation.*

According to the prophecies of Malachy there are only two popes remaining on a list that has spanned seven centuries. The next pope, according to Malachy, is "De Gloria Olivarum" meaning "From the glory of the Olive Tree." This could mean that the next pope would endure sufferings, since it reminds us of the Garden of Olives.

✤ ✤ ✤ ✤ ✤

Obstacle Two
The Olive Tree

There is another possible explanation. According to the *Boston Globe*, President Oscar Luigi Salfaro of Italy appointed Romano Prodi, Prime Minister, on May 16, 1996. Prodi, according to the *Globe*, is leader of the victorious center-left party called the "olive tree." The win brought former communists to power for the first time even in Italy.

The frightening thought is that the next pope may be put into power through the influence of communists. He could be the anti-Christ predicted in the *Book of Revelation*.

There is little doubt that the dire warnings given by Our Blessed Mother throughout the world seem to indicate a period of trails and tribulations.

The Era of Peace

The final pope in Malachy's list is called Petrus Romanus - Peter of Rome. Despite the fact that there has been 263 popes in the Roman Catholic Church, only St. Peter carried that name.

Does this mean the end of the world? Absolutely not! Our Blessed Mother promised at Fatima in 1917 that the Triumph of the Immaculate Heart of Mary would occur and it would be followed by an era of peace. We have seen that the Triumph of the Immaculate Heart of Mary would occur through her intercession. It is only the Holy Spirit that can bring about the era of peace and the desire of God the Father, manifested in the prayer of Jesus: "that they may be one, even as we are one."(John 17:11)

The Holy Father - A New Name?

Is it possible that the nomenclature of the head of the Catholic Church be changed? Could we call the head of the Catholic Church a name different than Pope? Pope John Paul, II makes it quite clear that we must all work to bring about unity in the church. Giving up a title such as Pope is not an insurmountable obstacle to the Holy Spirit. Perhaps the full title of Peter of Rome may be quite simple. He might be called, "Peter, Vicar of Jesus Christ, Patriarch of the West, Bishop of Rome, Beloved Brother."

This would be a small price to pay to enjoy reunion in the Catholic Church. Our present Holy Father wants more than anything to bring about the unity in the Church that Jesus so urgently desired. For the pontiff knows that Jesus wants only that "the will of God the Father be done on Earth as it is done in Heaven." When that happens the world will enjoy an era of peace, and through the powerful intercession of the Blessed Mother, the world will see the Triumph of the Immaculate Heart of Mary.

[1] Pope John Paul, II, *Tertio Millennio Adveniente,* (Boston, MA.: Pauline Books & Media, 1994), page 53, #49.

[2] *Catechism of the Catholic Church*, (New York: Catholic Book Publishing Co., 1992), pages 633-634, #2634.

[3] (*Catechism of the Catholic Church*, pages 636, #2647.)

[4] (Pope John Paul, II, *Tertio Millennio Adveniente,* page 57, #55.)

[5] United States National Headquarters of the Marian Movement of Priests, *Our Lady speaks to her Beloved Priests* (St. Francis, Maine, 1990). Page 918, Number 545.

[6] Staff writer for *Garabandal*, "The Warning and Miracle: Interviews with the seers" *Garabandal October-December 1984*, (Lindenhurst, N.Y.), page 12.

[7] Serre, Jacques, "They saw the Miracle" *Garabandal October-December 1984*, (Lindenhurst, N.Y.), page 24.

[8] (Ibid, page 24.)

[9] (Staff writer for *Garabandal*, pages 19 & 28.)

[10] (United States National Headquarters of the Marian Movement of Priests, page 930, Number 546.)

[11] Verheylezoon, Fr. Louis, *Devotion to the Sacred Heart* (Rockford, Illinois: Tan Books and Publishers, Inc.), page xxiii - xxiv.

[12] (Pope John Paul, II, *Tertio Millennio Adveniente,* page 44, #37.)

[13] Pope John Paul, II, *Ut Unum Sint,* (Boston, MA.: Pauline Books & Media, 1994), page 17, #5.

[14] Monyhan, Robert and Antoneo Gaspari "Can the Papacy Change" *Inside the Vatican June - July 1995.*

[15] (Pope, John Paul, II *Ut Unum Sint,* page 18, #6.)

[16] (Ibid, pages 20-21, #9.)

[17] (Ibid, page 21, #9.)

[18] (Ibid, page 23, #11.)

[19] (Ibid, pages 23-24, 12-13.)

[20] (Ibid, page 33, #21.)

[21] (Ibid, page 34, #22.)

[22] (Ibid, page 102, #95.)

[23] (Ibid, page 103, #95.)
[24] (Ibid, page 109, #102.)
[25] (Pope John Paul, II, *Tertio Millennio Adveniente*, page 44, #37.)
[26] (Ibid, page 43, #37.)

THE TRIUMPH OF OUR LADY

Section Five
The Year 2000
The Triumph of Our Lady

"Unity, after all, is a gift of the Holy Spirit"[1]
(Pope John Paul, II)

"... since Christ is the only way to the Father, in order to highlight His living and saving presence in the Church and the world, the International Eucharistic Congress will take place in Rome, on the occasion of the Great Jubilee. The Year 2000 will be intensely Eucharistic:..."[2]
(Pope John Paul, II)

Chapter One
The Era of Peace -- A Time of Unity

"It is essential not only to continue along the path of dialogue on doctrinal matters, but above all to be more committed to prayer for Christian unity. ... In unison with the great petition of Christ before his passion: 'Father... that they also may be one in us' (John 17:21)."[3]
(Pope John Paul, II)

✟✟✟✟✟

Advice of Our Lady

At Cana in Galilee it was Our Blessed Mother who was told that they had run out of wine. Immediately she acted as the intercessor. Our Lady's intercession was so incredibly gentle. "They have no more wine" (John 2:3). You would have expected a different response than Mary received. "Woman, (not Mother), how does this concern of yours involve Me? My hour has not yet come" (John 2:4).

Mary doesn't argue with her Son, or cajole Him. She simply told the wine stewards: "Do whatever He tells you" (John 2:5). Our Lady knew Jesus could never say "No" to His mother! I believe this is equally true today. Jesus will listen to her intercession. That is the meaning of the power of the "Triumph of the Immaculate Heart of Mary."

After the exciting weekend of intercessory prayer with Kathleen Keefe on May 3-4, 1996, and a day of recollection, I was elated that everything had gone so well. It had been a time of great grace. Having been invited to the IHS convention on Unity in Philadelphia on June 23, I decided to write this book primarily for pastors who may not be prepared for the coming of the third millennium.

When I returned from my day off on Monday to Slidell, I learned that one of my parishioners, an eighteen year old, had been arrested for murder. Then I began thinking of the eighth grade student two months ago who had been desecrating the Blessed Sacrament. What right did I have to speak at a national conference on "parish unity."

We are similar to every other parish in the country. Despite our attempts to do what Our Lady asked, our Mass attendance is discouraging. Only 2500 adults and children attend Sunday Mass out of a potential of 6500. One third of our CCD and parochial school students seldom go to Mass. I felt like the prophet Elijah who defeated the false prophets of Baal only to run away out of fear of Jezebel. But Our Blessed Mother seems to know exactly how to get me to do what she wants.

Not able to sleep, I got up only to discover that Kathleen had left her Bible in my rectory. Picking it up I discovered a piece of paper marking a spot in the Old Testament. It was the prophet, Jeremiah chapter 30. Since I am not one of those gifted with words of knowledge, I never expect scripture to confirm God's will for me. If only........

I began to read in the *Jerusalem Edition Bible*, much to my amazement.

> "Thus says the Lord, the God of Israel: **Write all the words I have spoken to you in a book.** For behold, the days will come, says the Lord, when I will change the lot of My people (of Israel and Judah, says the Lord), and bring them back to the land which I gave to their fathers; they shall have it as their possession."

It has been clear to me that our community has been led by the Holy Spirit to help others prepare for the Triumph of Our Lady and the victory of Jesus Christ. But I was excited to be told by the Lord to "write a book".

The second thing that struck me about this text was that it was exactly what Our Lady had said to my heart before and after my acute aortic dissection, "**As long as I am near you,**" Mary said, "**what do you have to fear?**"

> Jeremiah put it this way,
> "These are the words which the Lord spoke to Israel and Judah: thus says the Lord: 'A cry of dismay we hear; **fear reigns, not peace**. Inquire, and see: since when do men bear children? Why, then, do I see all these men, with their hands on their loins like women in childbirth? Why have all their faces turned deathly pale?'"
> (Jeremiah 30:4-6)

I am one of the most fearful people I know. However, in three years time Our Lady has led me through fearful experiences and yet gave me incredible peace. This happened when I was in the hospital in 1994 and faced life-threatening surgery in 1995 as well as the loss of my voice as a result of the surgery.

Incidentally, the message Jesus gave to Sister Faustina was exactly the same - not to fear. The prayer the Lord gave to this holy nun was, "Jesus, I trust in you."

The third surprise was the clarity of Jeremiah's prophecy - the tribulations that precede the era of peace will be devastating, but the remnant will survive. Jeremiah writes: "**How mighty is that day** (a day is a period of time, not 24 hours) -- **none like it!** A time of distress for Jacob, though he shall be saved from it." (Jeremiah 30:7).

The fourth message was that the chains of Satan will be broken. These chains include the addictions of sin, as well as the powerful hold Satan has over souls through pride, ignorance, atheism and communism. Jeremiah put it this way: "On that day, says the Lord of hosts, 'I will break his yoke from off your necks and snap your bonds.' Strangers shall no longer enslave them; ..." (Jeremiah 30:8).

On of the greatest chains that bind us is **shame**. Jesus destroyed that bondage on Calvary. We are free ... free at last of shame. We need to recognize that these chains will not be broken easily. I felt that the quotations from the Holy Father concerning martyrdom were extremely important. It may well be that the price of breaking this bondage may be the martyrdom of the faithful. The pope points out that every denomination and branch of Christianity is suffering martyrdom. The blood of these martyrs may help release the chains of the evil one as it did in the early church.

The Father's Will -- The Reign of Jesus Christ

Jeremiah prophesies how the era of peace will occur. The prophet writes: "**Instead, they shall serve the Lord, their God and David, their king, whom I will raise up for them.**" (Jeremiah 30:9). Can you imagine a day when everyone will serve the Lord our God? It sounds like the very prayer of Jesus in the "Our Father ... Thy kingdom come, thy will be done on earth as it is in heaven".

The descendant of David who is enthroned as king is clearly Jesus Christ. The prophet Jeremiah is speaking of the return of Jesus Christ as King of the universe. When this occurs, the very structure of the Church might be different if Jesus reigns in our hearts! When every human believes what Jesus taught, that he is truly present in the Eucharist, Christ will truly reign!

Those who are familiar with the apparitions of Garabandal know that Our Lady spoke of a great Eucharistic miracle. This great miracle would be Eucharistic, Marian, and ecclesial. It will lead people to the Church. It is to occur on the feast of a Eucharistic martyr, in the months of March, April, or May.

The Era of Peace

Jeremiah's final word to us is to forsake fear and know that we will live in peace. This is the era of peace promised by Our Blessed Mother at Fatima in 1917. Jeremiah writes: "But you, my servant Jacob, **fear not, says the Lord, be not dismayed, O Israel!** Behold, I will deliver you from the far-off land, your descendants, from their land of exile; Jacob shall again find rest, shall be tranquil and undisturbed, ..." (Jeremiah 30:10).

✞✞✞✞✞

The Warning of Christ

As we look forward to the era of peace, it is important to remember the warning of Christ in Sacred Scripture: "No man knows the day or the hour". Although we hope and pray that Father Gobbi's message is accurate, that the Triumph of Our Lady will take place before the end of the year 2000, the time table for both the cross and the glory is for God to decide.

We need to redouble our prayer and fasting as Our Lady has asked repeatedly at Medjugorje. Jesus also warned us that there will only be a remnant who remain faithful. "When the Son of Man comes, will He find any faith on the Earth?" (Luke 18:8) he asked rhetorically.

My plea is for expectant faith based on love. I pray that as a little child you will see in your mind's eye God as your loving Father. I hope that God the Son will become real to you in the person of Jesus Christ, as your Lord and Savior. I dream that each of you will come to experience the power and presence of the Holy Spirit, the Third Person of the Trinity.

The only way you can have expectant faith is to become like little children. Jesus said, "I assure you, unless you change and become like little children, you will not enter the kingdom of God." (Matthew 18:3) If you are a child or have the faith of a little child, mysteries don't disturb you. You know they were revealed to you by God, your loving Father, for a reason. You just blindly accept them.

Every year I give First Holy Communion to the members of our second grade, both in the CCD and the parochial school. One of the privileges I cherish as a pastor, is the right to give the Eucharist to my children for the first time. I do not delegate this privilege unless I am ill.

There is such an expectant faith in the eyes of each of these little ones. They have no doubt... it is Jesus they receive in Holy Communion. He said it ...I believe it... therefore it is true. That expectant faith lifts my spirits.

Intellectual Pride

Sometimes intellectuals have difficulty with faith. That is why so many scientists don't believe in the very existence of God. They constantly try to constrain God, to put Him in their test tubes. It's not that God is too remote to be believable, He is all around us, but He doesn't fit comfortably in the little boxes or the tiny crevices of the intellectuals' brains.

Fr. Gallagher, my elderly associate from Ireland, tells a wonderful story about a very, very smart priest. It seems that this priest was sent to Rome to study and he received a great number of degrees - Phd's Std., Stl. and was truly a smart, smart man. When the priest returned to Ireland, his bishop decided to send the smart, smart priest to a very small parish, perhaps in the hopes of teaching him humility. In his first sermon the priest told these poor peasants of all of the learning he had received and of his many degrees he had garnered. "I certainly hope," he said, "that you will contribute in an appropriate fashion to my upkeep." Two elderly Irishmen left church. Pat asked Mike, "Well, what do you think of the new priest?" "Ah, Pat" he replied, "He truly is a smart, smart man. But for the likes of us, I think we could have used a much dumber priest."

Unity -- The Work of the Holy Spirit

Our Holy Father put it best: "Unity, after all, is a gift of the Holy Spirit." The era of peace will result in Church unity - One, Holy, Catholic and Apostolic. With childlike faith, we can imagine that the causes of division will break down when each of us takes Jesus at his word. Just as in the case of the Eucharist, you can't change people's minds by the strength of intellectual arguments. But the Holy Spirit will change people's hearts. The problems will disappear and there will be unity in our homes, our parish and in the Church itself.

Our Catholic communities are being asked by the Holy Spirit to become intercessors, prayer warriors. Even a child can accept the words of Jesus when He told us of His great love for God the Father. Jesus said that God the

Father "... wants all men to be saved and come to know the truth." (1 Timothy 2:4)

Our parishes are also being asked to become centers of Divine Mercy. When you experience Divine Mercy in your own life through a mini judgment or illumination, your life will change. When you recognize that Jesus has carried your shame on Calvary and asked God the Father to forgive you, "For you knew not what you were doing," you too will want to be a disciple of mercy.

A Childlike Expectant Faith Demands Love

Jesus said: "If you love me ... obey the commands I give you, ..." (John 14:15) St. Paul tells us: "... God makes all things work together for the good of those who love God...." (Romans 8:28)

In childlike faith we must believe that the Holy Spirit wants to give us His greatest gift, His greatest charism - and that is love. St. Theresa of Avila said, "Humility cannot exist without love and detachment from created things."

Many have robbed their children by giving them "everything they didn't have as a child." What your children need is love... not things.

Angels with Only One Wing

I began this book with a desire to share with my brother priests what our community has learned about preparing for the third millennium and the Triumph of the Immaculate Heart of Mary and the era of peace. We built on a foundation of Eucharistic adoration, love of Our Lady, obedience to the Holy Father, and intercessory prayer of our children.

We strove to make Jesus the Lord of our lives, and to experience the power of the Holy Spirit. Evangelization was a call to answer God the Father's desire for the salvation of all men. We know now from experience that Divine Mercy changes hearts and intercessory prayer works. We have an expectant faith that great works of healing will one day flourish, for we have seen the effect of inner healing.

In a talk I once gave at a Confirmation retreat for our high school seniors, I explained each of us are "angels with only one wing." I told them that each of us is given some charism or gift of the Holy Spirit. This charism is like the wing of an angel. Since we have only one wing, we cannot fly; however, if we join our wings together, we can soar like angels. Our Sunday night choir director, Mark Hargrave, wrote a song entitled "Angels With Only One Wing".

We can all become true intercessors - Charismatics, Marianists, Marriage Encounter, Cursillo - if we recognize that each group is given only one wing. By yourselves you will crash and destroy your parish community, but if you join together with other spirit filled groups, your parish will truly soar. You can not fly with only one wing.

Parishes -- Models of Love

In St. John's gospel chapter 15:13-14, he tells us that "God is love". Jesus modeled love for us when he said: "There is no greater love than this: to lay down one's life for one's friends. You are my friends if you do what I command you."

This era will be a time of great evangelization. As millions accept Jesus as Lord and Savior, they will become messengers of Divine Mercy. As important as doctrinal and scriptural knowledge is, we must remember that the early church was spread by the example of the members. For people said of them: "See how they love one another."

I love the story of the abbot who was quite discouraged. Few young men were entering the monastery. One day he went out into the woods to pray and there he met a rabbi. "Can you give me any advice?" the abbot pleaded. "Tell them the messiah is among them," the rabbi replied. The abbot reported the conversation to the remaining monks. They were astonished. Surely it couldn't be this one or that one... but who knows? So the monks began to treat each monk as if he truly was the Lord. Word began to spread.. Jesus is here... He is among us! Young and old flocked to join. The number grew beyond measure.

One day all of our people will become aware of the truth. Jesus is alive, He is present among us! When that happens, the world will flock to our Catholic Churches. "Come, Lord Jesus, come!"

Chapter Two
Triumph of Our Lady

"I entrust this responsibility of the whole Church to the maternal intercession of Mary, Mother of the Redeemer. She, the Mother of Fairest Love, will be for Christians on the way to the Great Jubilee of the Third Millennium the Star which safely guides their steps to the Lord. May the unassuming young woman of Nazareth, who two thousand years ago offered to the world the Incarnate Word, lead the men and women of the new millennium towards the One who is 'the true light that enlightens every man' (Jn 1:9)."[4]
(Pope John Paul, II)

Our Lady of Guadalupe told Father Gobbi of the Marian movement of priests, "I confirm to you that, by the Great Jubilee of the year two thousand, there will take place the Triumph of my Immaculate Heart, of which I foretold you at Fatima, and this will come to pass with the return of Jesus in glory to establish His reign in the world. Then you will at last be able to see with your own eyes the new heavens and the new earth."[5] This message was received by Father Gobbi at the shrine of Our Lady of Guadalupe, Mexico City on December 5, 1994.

The Triumph of the Immaculate Heart of Mary was first announced by Our Lady at Fatima on July 13, 1917 when Mary told the children, "In the end, my Immaculate Heart will triumph. The Holy Father will consecrate Russia to me, she will be converted, and an era of peace will be granted to the world."[6] The Triumph of Our Lady is through intercession.

Sacred Scripture gives us a wonderful example of the Triumph of the Immaculate Heart of Mary. In the *Book of Esther* in the Old Testament, King Ahasuerus of Persia had decided to annihilate the Jewish people the thirteenth day of the month. Queen Esther interceded before the king to save the Jewish people.

Our Blessed Mother interceded before her son, Jesus, to prevent the destruction of the world. Just as Esther appeared on the 13th day of the month, Our Blessed Mother appeared at Fatima, Portugal, to the visionaries on the 13th of the month. "Esther" means "star". When Mary appeared at Fatima she wore a star on her dress, which suggest the analogy.

Haman appears in the *Book of Esther* as the individual who plots the destruction of the Jews like Satan plots the annihilation of nations. However, Queen Esther intercedes to prevent the destruction of the Jews, just as Our Lady will prevent the annihilation of the world if people respond to her requests.

Queen Esther asked the Jewish people to fast and pray to prevent their destruction. Our Blessed Mother requested the collegial consecration by the Pope and all Bishops to her Immaculate Heart. Mary requested the First Saturday Devotion of Confession and Communion, Rosary, and Meditation. Because of Mary's intercession Jesus will grant us His mercy, just as King Ahasuerus did for Queen Esther. As a result of Mary's intervention, we will be given a period of peace just as the Persian King did for Queen Esther. This will result in the Triumph of the Immaculate Heart of Mary and the return of Jesus Christ as Eucharistic Lord.[7]

The Triumph of the Immaculate Heart of Mary, the prevention of world annihilation and Mary's promised period of peace began with the Holy Father's collegial consecration of the world to her Immaculate Heart on March 25, 1984. It is our hope that it will culminate in the near future.

✝✝✝✝✝

Triumph of Our Lady

Many of the aspects of the Holy Spirit's plan to bring about the Triumph of Our Lady have been shown to us. It can be summarized as follows:

1. **Divine Mercy** - Under the patronage of Blessed Faustina. We can accept Jesus as Lord only when we:
    A. See ourselves as sinners -- illumination or mini judgment
    B. Seek repentance through the Sacrament of Penance.
    C. Seek reconciliation through the power of the Holy Spirit.
    D. Use the tools of the Holy Spirit, especially humility.

2. **Discipleship** - Jesus Christ must become Lord of our lives. We become a fully armed disciple by prayer, adoration of the Blessed Sacrament, evangelization, study of the Bible and the teachings of the Catholic Church, empowerment of the Holy Spirit, and exercising the charisms of the Holy Spirit.

3. **Become intercessors for the universal church** - Under the patronage of Padre Pio. We can bring about her triumph by becoming true intercessors praying for unity of the church.
    A. Priests and Laymen -- through suffering and prayer.
    B. Catholics and non-Catholics, Orthodox, Jews, Muslims and all unbelievers -- through prayer, suffering and martyrdom.

Mary - Our Mother Introduces Us

Strangely, sometimes as we read Scriptures, it is as if it were the first time. Reading the gospel for the feast of the presentation of Jesus in the temple (Luke 2:22-40), touched my heart. I know that Our Lady is teaching our community the importance of intercession. As our intercessor, Mary will do even more for us; she will introduce us to the heavenly father.

The thought immediately hit me; Simeon's prayer is the same as each of us who long for the coming of Jesus Christ in glory. **"Lord I want to see your return in power"** we want to witness as Simeon said: "For my eyes have witnessed you saving deed displayed for all the peoples to see: A revealing light to the Gentiles, the glory of your people Israel." (Luke 2:30-32)

I pray to live through the trials Our Blessed Mother has predicted to see the era of true peace. The confidence I have that we will weather the worst storm comes from the realization that this community will accept in childlike submission whatever Our Blessed Mother tells us to do.

The cast of characters who were there at the presentation in the temple are even now assembling for the battle of Armageddon. Malachi 2:17 is an answer to a question that the prophet Malachi posed to himself "where is the just God?" This reading is used by the Church at the Feast of the Presentation of Jesus in the Temple.

His answer is just as valid today as it was for those anxiously awaiting the first coming of the Messiah. **"And suddenly there will come to the temple, the Lord whom**

you seek." (Malachi 3:1) The presentation of Jesus in the temple was the fulfillment of that prophesy.

However, there is a deeper more ominous message. The second coming of Christ in power will be preceded by a messenger. It is an angel who has a warning for us. "But who will endure the day of His coming? And who can stand when He appears? For He is like the refiner's fire, or like the fuller's lye. He will sit refining and purifying [silver], and He will purify the sons of Levi, refining them like gold or like silver...." (Malachi 3:2-3) This is clearly similar to the warning given by Christ himself: "But when the Son of Man comes, will He find any faith on the earth?" (Luke 18:8)

The prophet explains in Malachi 3:5 the reason some have to fear the day of the Lord: "I will draw near to you for judgment and I will be swift to bear witness against the sorcerers, adulterers, and perjurers, those who defraud the hired man of his wages, against those who defraud widows and orphans; those who turn aside the stranger, and those who do not fear me, says the Lord of hosts." Incidentally the sorcerer is one who is involved in the demonic.

So one of the characters in the drama is an angel. One sign I see in St. Margaret Mary Community is a renewed devotion to the angels, particularly our guardian angels. Some of my children have seen angels in our church. In other communities and schools angels will simply be dismissed as childish mythology.

Hebrews 2:14-15 identifies the adversary. It is Satan! The author of Hebrews tells us "Now, since the children are men of blood and flesh, Jesus likewise had a full share in ours, that by His death He might rob the devil, the prince of death, of his power and free those who through fear of death had been slaves their whole life long." This promise is equally valid today. There are countless souls addicted to drugs, sex, violence, alcohol, gambling and a host of other addictions. The Divine Mercy will certainly have a cleansing effect on many. Our Blessed Mother tells us at Medjugorje that after the tenth sign is revealed there will be a period of intense conversion, which will be very brief.

Sadly many will dismiss Satan as another childish symbol. It is interesting that Pope Paul, VI complained during his lifetime that the "smoke of Satan had infiltrated even the Vatican." One of my spiritual daughters was fired from her volunteer teaching position in a parish CCD program because she was teaching the children that Satan exists. Sad isn't it? One of the signs of the remnant community will be a clear knowledge that Satan is real, he exists and he is the enemy.

St. Luke tells us of the other main characters in the drama of the presentation. In addition to Jesus we have Mary and the Holy Spirit. We have young people and adults who can be witness to the power of the Holy Spirit. His presence will certainly be a key to the peace that you should feel in this community. It is one of the tasks of the Holy Spirit to cast out fear. **A remnant community must be without fear**. You notice it was the Holy Spirit who opened the eyes of Simeon to the presence of Jesus. It will be the Holy Spirit who opens our eyes to the power of Christ.

Our Blessed Mother is a key player in this drama. In the Second Vatican Council the Church added to the multitude of titles accorded her by declaring her the Mother of the Church.

Many individuals casually dismiss the countless efforts Our Blessed Mother has made to warn us of these dangerous times. Only a mother would exert the efforts she had made to awaken us to the real danger of our times by appearing throughout the world.

For a few days a couple of years ago we had a replica of the cloak of Our Lady of Guadalupe. The image of Our Lady had been left on the cloak of Juan Diego in Mexico in 1531. At the time 20,000 infants were being killed each year. The superstitious Indians were cutting out their hearts and using them in human sacrifice. Our Lady has asked that this replica be sent throughout the Americas to warn us of the horrors of abortion. The replicas have been the source of great grace. It is hoped that it will melt any hearts in any community that do not have a great love for Mary, Our Mother.

In chapter 12 of the Book of Revelation, sacred scripture gives us an insight into the battle in which we are engaged. "A great sign appeared in the sky, a woman clothed with the sun, with the moon under her feet, and on her head a crown of twelve stars." This is the visualization that you see in the statue of Our Lady in St. Margaret Mary Church.

In Revelation 12:7-10 the Bible sets the stage: "Then war broke out in heaven; Michael and his angels battled against the dragon. Although the dragon and his angels fought back, they were overpowered and lost their place in heaven. ... Then I heard a loud voice in heaven say: 'Now have salvation and power come, the reign of our God and the authority of his Anointed One."

In Genesis 3:15 we are told of the enmity between Satan and the woman (Mary). "He (Satan) will strike at your head, while you (Mary) strike at his heel." It will be the heel of Mary that in God's providence will crush the serpent Satan.

The dream I have for each of us, is that we like Christ in the gospel will be carried in the arms of our mother. It will be Mary herself who will present us to the heavenly father. Another word for presentation is introduction. It will be Mary who will introduce us. She will acknowledge us as her sons and daughters.

The scapular of Our Lady and the rosary are two clear signs that you belong to Mary and hence to Jesus. Just as it was the scapular of a child that prevented Pope John Paul, II from being killed on the feast of the anniversary of Our Lady of Fatima, on May 13, 1981[8], so too will you be protected during the coming trails. Some outside the remnant community will make fun of the scapular as superstitious. Make no mistake about the power of Our Mother and those she protects.

Enrollment in the Scapular

For many years, all of the children at St. Margaret Mary have been enrolled in the brown scapular of Our Lady of Mt. Carmel when they make their First Communion. On the Feast of the Assumption of Our Lady, August 15, 1996, all adults who attended Mass were enrolled in the Third Order of Mt. Carmel. They each received a blessed scapular of Our Lady.

In 1980, according to Malachi Martin, Pope John Paul, II spoke about the fact that we were living in the era of punishment foretold at Fatima, Portugal in 1917. When asked about the trials, the Holy Father said they were going to occur. "Is there anything we can do?" "Yes," the Pope responded, "say your rosary, this will lessen the trials." Yet there are many Catholics who mock this devotion.

It is also significant that the Holy Father realizes that he is under the protection of Our Lady. The Pope prays the consecration to the Immaculate Heart by Saint Louis De

Monforte daily. The motto of the Holy Father, "Totus Tuus" or "totally yours" says it all. Our parish recites the consecration after all daily Masses.

Consecration

These childlike devotions, daily consecration, the rosary and the scapular may be mocked by many. However, when the battle is raging with Satan, I hope each of you will be warned by the Holy Spirit, protected by the angels and find yourselves comfortably ensconced in the arms of Our Lady. What a joy it will be to hear her say to the Heavenly Father, "I would like to present my son/daughter to you." Our Lady will not only intercede for us. She will be the one who will introduce us to the Heavenly Father.

Chapter Three
The Eucharist

*"The year 2000 will be intensely Eucharistic: in
the Sacrament of the Eucharist the Savior, who took flesh
in Mary's womb twenty centuries ago, continues to offer
Himself to humanity as the source of divine life."[9]*
(Pope John Paul, II)

The Last Heresy - The Denial of the Real Presence

We know that Our Blessed Mother has warned us
as early as Fatima in 1917, and again at Medjugorje of trials
that will beset the Church. Fr. Gobbi as simple Italian priest
has been used by Our Blessed Mother to form the Marian
Movement of Priests worldwide. Our Lady gave us this
warning in a message to Fr. Gobbi at Malvern,
Pennsylvania, November 15, 1990, "I announce to you the
moment of divine justice and great mercy has now arrived.
You will know the hour of weakness and of poverty; the
hour of suffering and defeat; the purifying hour of great
chastisement."

I believe that in the time of trial, the last heresy will
be the denial of the real presence of Jesus in the Eucharist.
The great hope of the Church will be the Remnant
Communities - those who not only believe in the real
presence of Jesus in the Eucharist; but demonstrate that
belief by Perpetual Adoration of the Blessed Sacrament.

As I reflected on the history of the Catholic Church,
my mind went back to the time of the Great Schism in the
Catholic Church in the sixteenth century - The Protestant
Revolt or "Reformation." It was something that I had read
when I was on my sabbatical from the *Story of Civilization*
by Will and Ariel Durant. I found this quotation:

"Petrarch lamented the fact that in the minds of many scholars it was a sign of ignorance to prefer the Christian religion to pagan philosophy. In Venice (1530), it was found that most of the upper ranks neglected their Easter Duties. Luther claimed to have found a saying current among the educated classes in Italy on going to Mass; 'Come let us conform to the popular error' ... Erasmus was astonished to find that at Rome, the fundamentals of the Christian faith were topics of skeptical discussion among the Cardinals. One ecclesiastic undertook to explain to him the absurdity of belief in a future life, others smiled at Christ and the Apostles. Many, he assures us, claimed to have heard Papal functionaries blaspheming the Mass. The lower class kept their faith as we shall see. The thousands who heard Savonorola must have believed, but the soul of the Great Creed had been pierced with arrows of doubt."[10]

Simply put, a failure to believe in the Eucharist was one of the major causes for the Protestant Reformation. The division within the Church was a result of a lack of belief in the Real Presence of Jesus Christ in the Eucharist. It was the faith of the poor that saved the Church in the sixteenth century. History is soon to repeat itself.

Those of us old enough to remember the Catholic church before 1962 are astonished by the lack of belief in the real presence today. We have lived through a time that Catholics who formerly went to Mass every Sunday no longer consider their absence on Sunday a mortal sin. Certainly they have convinced themselves that missing Mass will not result in eternal damnation...if they still believe in an after life.

In 1960, nearly ninety percent of American Catholics attended Mass regularly. That percentage today is about thirty percent. In many parts of Europe only ten percent of the people go to Mass.

As disturbing as it is to contemplate the many who fail to attend Sunday Mass, an equally great scandal is the number who receive Holy Communion in the state of mortal sin. Individuals who have not gone to confession for years, would never think of passing up Holy Communion. Individuals who have intellectual problems with the Immaculate Conception, and wonder how God could have allowed His own Mother to be conceived free from all sin (Immaculate Conception), suddenly convince themselves that they are free from all sin. In most parishes, the few who brave the confessional are a testament that not all deny the efficacy of the Sacrament of Penance.

The final heresy is that so many no longer believe that it is Jesus present in the Eucharist under the appearance of bread and wine. The words of Jesus (John 6:52-54) are simple and clear; "Let me solemnly assure you, if do not eat the flesh of the Son of Man and drink His blood, you have no life in you. He who feeds on my flesh and drinks my blood has life eternal and I will raise him up on the last day."

Unfortunately, there are many Catholics who have lost their faith, think of Holy Communion as a pious custom and give lip service to the teachings of Jesus Christ and His Church. St. Paul warns in I Corinthians 11:27:
"This means that whoever eats the bread or drinks the cup of the Lord unworthily sins against the body and blood of the Lord. ... He who eats and drinks without recognizing the body eats and drinks a judgment on himself."

The scandals of the Eucharist abound today. How many people would leave Mass early - immediately after Communion if they believed in the Real Presence of Jesus Christ? By faith we know it is at that moment that Jesus is most present to us, yet we see people hurrying to get to their cars as if they had something more important to do.

Someone recently told of a priest announcing at a wedding, "Any Protestants who want to receive Communion today may do so." This is clearly a scandal, as it distorts Catholic teaching. St. Paul writes, "This means that whoever eats the bread or drinks the cup of the Lord unworthily sins against the body and blood of the Lord." (1 Corinthians 11:27) The Eucharist is not to be given simply because we don't want to offend people of other faiths. In our community we yearn for the day that the mystical body of Christ will be one. We invite those unable to receive Holy Communion to come forward and receive a blessing, which is tantamount to communion of desire. Watering down Catholic doctrine will not bring about unity in the Church.

✚✚✚✚✚

You are a Remnant Church

Those Catholic Communities that believe in the True Presence of Jesus in the Eucharist are remnant churches. Your faith is as simple as that of a child ... Jesus said, " This is my body...This is my blood;" as a community they believe this with all their hearts.

The window in the front entrance at St. Margaret Mary is a constant reminder of the Cross and the Eucharist. There is a cross in red, with the Eucharist in the center of that Crucifix. Jesus is Lord of our lives when we accept Him as Savior and follow His instructions, when He told the apostles at the Last Supper, " Do this as a remembrance of

Me." (Luke 22:10) Jesus wanted more than lip service. We prove our belief in the Eucharist, not only by attending Sunday Mass but by attending daily Mass as well. We prove our belief in the Real Presence of Jesus in the Eucharist by our hour of Adoration of the Blessed Sacrament each week.

At Malvern, Pennsylvania, Our Blessed Mother told Father Gobbi, "You have also wished to make more intense your Act of Love and reparation to Jesus present in the Most Holy Eucharist by nocturnal adoration so pleasing to me and blessed by me, because it has given great comfort and joy to the Eucharistic and Priestly Heart of Jesus.

The Year 2000 - Intensely Eucharistic

The Holy Father, Pope John Paul II, explains why the Great Jubilee in the year 2000 must be Eucharistic: "... the *Great Jubilee*, which will take place simultaneously in the Holy Land, in Rome, and in local churches throughout the world. Especially in this phase, the *phase of celebration*, the aim will be *to give glory to the Trinity*, from whom everything in the world and in history comes and to whom everything returns." ... "But since Christ is the only way to the Father, in order to highlight His living and saving presence in the Church and the world, *the International Eucharistic Congress* will take place in Rome, on the occasion of the Great Jubilee. The year 2000 will be intensely Eucharistic: in the *Sacrament of the Eucharist* the savior, who took flesh in Mary's womb twenty centuries ago, continues to offer Himself to humanity as the source of divine life"[11]

How Will Reunion Occur?

It is evident that reunion of the church that was split asunder in the sixteenth century between Protestant and Catholics is possible only by the power of the Holy Spirit.

The Holy Father makes that perfectly clear in his encyclicals, *Ut Unum Sint* (That they may be one) and *Tertio Millennio Adveniente* (On the Coming of the Third Millennium).

We have the promise of Our Blessed Mother at Fatima in 1917 that an era of peace would occur, after the consecration of Russia to the Immaculate Heart of Mary. This was done by Pope John Paul II together with the Bishops in 1984.

Our Lady told the children in Garabandal, Spain (1961 - 1965), that a great Eucharistic miracle would occur in our lifetime. This seems to be the same miracle Mary spoke of in Medjugorje. This miracle will occur, we are told, on a Marian feast of a martyr for the Eucharist.

✠✠✠✠✠

The Return of Jesus Christ as Eucharistic Lord

I believe that the return of Jesus Christ will be to reign in the hearts of all men as Eucharistic Lord. The Eucharistic miracle promised by Our Blessed Mother will result in a great renewal of faith in the Catholic Church.

The division in the Church in the sixteenth century was a punishment from God the Father, for a lack of belief in the Real Presence of Christ in the Eucharist. The great Miracle promised by Our Lady at Garabandal will be Eucharistic. Belief in the teachings of Jesus Christ on the Eucharist will be the cornerstone of renewal that will result in the unity Jesus prayed from before his death. Imagine for a moment what it will be like when every Christian truly believes that Jesus Christ is truly present at every mass throughout the world. The unity of the church will once again become a reality.

The final heresy will be defeated. Jesus Christ will reign in the hearts of all throughout the world. This will reunite the entire church. Conversions will abound and Divine Mercy will cause incredible miracles of healing. Satan will be chained for a thousand years, and Christ will reign for a thousand years (Revelation 20:4).

The *Book of Revelation* should be our source of hope and not despair. In the end Jesus Christ will be the victor. Jesus will use His mother as a powerful tool of intercession. The Triumph of the Immaculate Heart of Mary will usher in a era of peace. The author of the *Book of Revelation* summarizes our trust - which is in Jesus alone. he writes: "The One who gives this testimony says, 'Yes, I am coming soon!' Amen! Come Lord Jesus!" (Revelation 22:20).

Chapter Four
God the Father's Will is Done Here on Earth as It is Done in Heaven

"The Jubilee, centered on the person of Christ, thus becomes a great act of praise to the Father."[12]
(Pope John Paul, II)

"A cloud came, overshadowing them, and out of the cloud a voice: 'This is My Son, My beloved. Listen to Him.'"
(Mark 9:7)

✝✝✝✝✝

Pentecost Sunday
A Unified Parish
May 26, 1996

On June 23, 1996, I was invited to give a talk entitled "The Unified Parish." The organizers of this Marian Conference were trying to bring together all of the spirit filled groups in the Catholic Church into a unified front against Satan. Due to an interest in my book, *The Remnant Church*, they felt I could address the issue of how to unify a parish.

In preparing for this talk I studied extensively the Pope's encyclical entitled *Tertio Millennio Adveniente* meaning "On the Coming of the Third Millennium." It is clear to me that the preparation for the year 2000 is the same type of preparation needed for the possibility of the Triumph of the Immaculate Heart of Mary predicted by Our Blessed Mother at Fatima in 1917. Her Immaculate Heart will triumph and an era of peace will occur.

In December, 1994, while at the Shrine of Our Lady of Guadelupe, Fr. Gobbi was told that the Triumph of Our

Lady and the Return of Jesus Christ will occur before the year 2000.

✝✝✝✝✝

Return of Jesus Christ -- A Promise

In a marvelous video, David Gant shares an extraordinary grace given to him. In 1992, while scuba diving with a friend in a cave on the Tennessee River near Alabama, David became trapped for 20 hours in a cave, in freezing water holding onto a stalactite. Finally he prayed, "Lord, save my soul."

David describes how a hand pulled out pure evil from him three times. The third time he began to shout and praise God. He was given the Baptism of the Holy Spirit. He was so joyful he prayed, "Lord, take me, take me."

"The Lord talked to me," David said. Jesus had a message: "**Get** your family ready for me. I will be back for my children before the year 2000. **Tell the whole world.**"[13]

A Sense of Urgency!

The Holy Father tells us that unity of the parish, the family, the church and the world can be accomplished "only by the Holy Spirit." So now you know why it is so necessary for us to have a relationship with the Holy Spirit. There are three important lessons to learn.

1.   Where will this power come from to bring about a world in which God the Father's will is done on Earth as it is in heaven? Clearly the answer is the Holy Spirit.

     In the reading from the *Acts of the Apostles*, you see a small band of apostles praying with Our Blessed

Mother. They are frightened, so they are hiding. As soon as the Holy Spirit comes into their lives "They began to express themselves in foreign tongues and make bold proclamation as the Spirit prompted them."(Acts 2:4) Three thousand were converted that one day. In the near future you too will witness amazing conversions through the power of the Holy Spirit.

2.   In order to be used by the Holy Spirit we must be prepared by Divine Mercy. The very first step to Divine Mercy, for Catholics, will be the Sacrament of Penance or Confession.

In St. John's Gospel chapter 20:21-23 you have the clear words of Jesus to his apostles and hence to all his priests:
> "'As the Father has sent me, so I send you.' Then he breathed on them and said: 'Receive the Holy Spirit. If you forgive men's sins, they are forgiven them; if you hold them bound, they are held bound.'"

There is much more to being open to Divine Mercy. Very soon each one of you will be given the same gift I received in 1994, which was spoken of by Our Lady at Garabandal and told to Sister Faustina by Jesus himself, "you will see yourself as God sees you." Incidentally David Gant, a Protestant who had a religious experience in a cave tells of seeing himself as God sees him. Only then did the hand of God reach deep inside him three times to remove the evil from his heart. Seeing yourself as God sees you is a gift of the Holy Spirit.

As I was recovering from surgery in October, 1995, I learned that confession alone is not sufficient. You must be reconciled with those who have hurt you, or the ones you have hurt. Jesus tells us in scripture: "If you bring your gift to the altar and there recall that your brother has anything against you, leave your gift at the altar, go first to be reconciled with your brother, and then come and offer your gift."(Matthew 5:23-24)

The third element of Divine Mercy is inner healing.

3.   The final thing we must do to be prepared for the return of Jesus Christ is to make Jesus the   Lord
of   our lives. We have been doing that for years in this community in the following manner:

     a.   You know that you are a sinner (c.f. confession) acknowledge your sinfulness and **accept Jesus as Lord and Savior.** Bill Bright from Campus Crusade has done a great job preaching this aspect of "being saved." However, for Catholics there is much more.

In the second reading, on Pentecost Sunday Paul's letter to the Corinthians says: **"And no one say, 'Jesus is Lord,' except in the Holy Spirit."** (1 Corinthians 12:3) That means we must be open to the power and gifts of the Holy Spirit. You receive the Holy Spirit in Baptism, as well as the Sacrament of Confirmation. You must stir up the graces that are already in you, and be open to the charisms and gifts of the Holy Spirit.

     b.   Jesus warned "none of those who cry out, 'Lord, Lord,' will enter the kingdom of God but only the one who does the **will of My Father in Heaven."**

We know the will of God the Father through the teachings of Jesus Christ in His Church.

Reception of Jesus in Holy Communion. Jesus said "unless you eat my flesh and drink My Blood, you will not have life in you." (John 6.) What good is it to say Jesus is Lord if you don't follow his command to "eat My Flesh and drink My Blood." Belief in the real presence of Jesus Christ is not a universal doctrine among Christians. Many Protestants believe the bread and wine are merely symbols. When they gave up the priesthood as they did, they sacrificed the most significant element to make Jesus the Lord of your life ... the reception of Jesus in Holy Communion.

How Will Jesus Christ Return in Glory?

"I saw one like a son of man coming, on the clouds of heaven; When he reached the Ancient One and was presented before him, He received dominion, glory, and kingship; nations and peoples of every language serve him. His dominion is an everlasting dominion that shall not be taken away, his kingship shall not be destroyed." (Daniel 7:13-14)

"It was not by way of cleverly concocted myths that we taught you about the coming in power of our Lord Jesus Christ, for we were eyewitnesses of his sovereign majesty. He received glory and praise from God the Father when that unique declaration came to him out of the majestic splendor: 'This is My beloved Son, and whom My favor rests.' ... Keep your attention closely fixed on it, as you would on a lamp shining in a dark place until the first streaks of dawn appear and the morning star rises in your hearts." (2 Peter 1:16-19)

It will be the Holy Spirit who will prepare the hearts of people to truly believe that Jesus Christ is

present in the Eucharist. You will live to experience a church divided for 500 years reunited and glorified when every Christian, Moslem and Jew, Pagan and Atheist knows Jesus is among us, present in the Eucharist. It is Jesus you adore in adoration of the Blessed Sacrament. It is Jesus you adore present at every Mass in Holy Communion.

Miracles Do Happen

I promised to tell you a story of a marvelous cure that began at intercessory prayer. Every Friday night since April we have been called to pray for unity in the family, the church and the world, through **intercessory prayer**. It begins at 7:00 p.m. and ends at 10:00 p.m. On the first Friday of the month, we omit some of the prayers and have a Mass of Inner Healing. It was at a Mass of Inner Healing that this miracle occurred through Divine Mercy. Jesus cured a woman of shame. Incidentally Jesus, during his lifetime, cured more people of shame than he did of physical ailments. Hopefully these stories will open the hearts of some of my children to realize that we are now in the time of great mercy and the time of tribulation. Mary's children will be protected and miracles will abound. In less than four years time you will enjoy the era of peace she prophesied in 1917 in Fatima. Here is the story.

The Holy Spirit Alone Heals Our Shame

One of our Parishioners told how the Holy Spirit had healed her of shame. A woman name Glaucia attended our inner healing Mass on the first Friday of May (May 4, 1996). Fr. Benson and his prayer team prayed over her after Mass. She felt an incredible warmth go through her body. Her chronic sinus problem, which caused her dizziness, was healed.

On the next day, Glaucia went to the chapel before the Blessed Sacrament to thank Jesus. It seemed as if "fire came from the Monstrance and went through my body," Glaucia said. She heard one very audible word ... **forgiveness**.

The more she thought about it, Glaucia realized it was her husband she needed to forgive. Thirteen years before, he had forced her to have an abortion. As a young married woman, Glaucia resisted to the point that she decided to kill herself.

Living in Rio de Janeiro at the time, she decided to drown herself rather than kill her baby. The lake there is quite deep and she couldn't swim. Just as she was about to jump into the lake, an elderly couple began to pass by. "I'll wait until they pass," Glaucia thought, "they don't deserve this painful memory."

It was a cloudy day. The elderly couple stopped and began to chat. It seemed they would never move. Finally, just as they passed, Glaucia looked up. The sky had cleared and the powerful image of Christ that dominates the hillside in Rio was visible. The outstretched hands of Christ touched her heart. She could not kill herself. She had a child in school who needed her.

When Glaucia returned home, her husband insisted that he would drive her to the abortion clinic. He dropped her off and the fetus was surgically removed. It would be years before Glaucia could forgive her husband.

After Glaucia had her encounter with the Lord in our chapel she realized that she must forgive her husband after thirteen years. She finally was able, by the grace of the Holy Spirit, to do so. That night in a dream, Glaucia saw her baby whom she had aborted. She had the experience of holding that child in her arms. She knew her baby was in heaven. All because she was able to forgive her husband. After the abortion it seemed it was impossible for her to give totally of herself to her husband. Now their relationship has improved in every aspect, as they grow closer to each other daily.

The next day Glaucia went back to the Blessed Sacrament chapel to thank Jesus for letting her see her baby and know she was in heaven. Once again she was given a powerful word ... "unnoticed." Glaucia thanked Jesus for the "unnoticed miracles."

Glaucia couldn't wait to get home. She had two large benign cysts on her breasts that were a cause for serious concern. When she returned home she discovered that the cysts were completely gone.

What is extraordinary to me it seems, is not the cure of her sinus or the removal of the cysts, but the cure of her shame. The Holy Spirit worked this miracle because Glaucia was willing to forgive her husband after thirteen years for forcing her to have an abortion. Forgiveness opens us up to the power of the Holy Spirit who alone can remove our shame. This miracle occurred because of intercessory prayer.

Intercessory Prayer: A Tool of Evangelization

During the month of July, 1996, I spoke to Lola Falana a famous entertainer who is a convert to the Catholic Church. During the summer of 1996, Ms. Falana was healed of a debilitating disease, multiple sclerosis, by Our Blessed Mother at Medjugorje. I asked Ms. Falana if she would give her testimony at our First Friday Mass of Inner Healing on September 6, 1996.

Lola readily agreed to give her testimony. She is literally on fire to evangelize. "I am disappointed" Lola said, "at the few numbers of black and brown sisters and brothers who attend these talks which I give at Marian

Conferences around the country." "I promise we will do our best to get a representation of all of God's children at St. Margaret Mary," I assured her. I realize that "division" is a tool of Satan. We are being divided by race and religion. The rich are set against the poor; the sick against the healthy; the old against the young. **Only the Holy Spirit can bring us unity**.

Lynn's Testimony on Divine Mercy

How can priests in a white suburban area heal the many divisions (racial, religious, and cultural) that plague our Church and our society? Both Fr. Benson and I gave sermons on racism on the sixteenth Sunday of Ordinary Times (July 20-21, 1996). The Gospel was on the weeds growing together with the wheat. How can we hope to root out racism without causing a mass exodus of white Catholics? How can we unite the church as one? We all seem to have our own prejudices. One of the great plagues of this era is AIDS. Do you see all victims of AIDS as sinners? Can the Church heal the hurts brought on by division? Clearly this can be accomplished only by the power of the Holy Spirit.

During my three sermons I shared the testimony "Lynn" had given at the previous Friday night intercessory prayer meeting. Lynn was deeply concerned how her testimony would be accepted but trusted in the Holy Spirit.

Lynn had been gang raped in her mid teens. She was later raped and stalked for three months in her early twenties. Her parents, who felt she was not as pretty as her sister, made no attempt to get her into counseling.

Lynn left the Catholic Church. She married an artist in a civil ceremony. They had two children. After twelve years she learned that her husband was involved in homosexuality and she got a divorce. Three years later she received a call from her husband; he had an advanced case of AIDS and was dying. When Lynn was tested she learned that she too had an advanced case of AIDS. Soon afterwards her ex-husband died. Her two children were not infected.

Lynn joined a support group and fell in love with a man who spoke of God changing his life and how scripture had consoled him. Desperate for love, Lynn married him in the Catholic Church. However, her new husband became seriously ill the evening of the wedding and died four months later, but not without telling her he still loved the woman that he knew before they had met.

On the Saturday before Divine Mercy Sunday, Lynn went to confession. Since then she has attended daily mass whenever she was able. Soon after this Lynn moved from Florida to Slidell, and ended up at St. Margaret Mary Parish.

In May, 1995, Lynn was hospitalized with a deadly form of pneumonia. Many AIDS patients die from this illness. Fr. Carroll came and administered the sacrament of the sick and she prayed constantly. During a special test in which she was to remain still for 20 minutes, she prayed to Jesus. It was 3:00 p.m., the hour of Divine Mercy.

Lynn asked for healing and began saying the Chaplet of Divine Mercy on her fingers. Within a matter of seconds, her head involuntarily jerked back, a popping sound came from her lungs and she began to breath clearly. Lynn knew she was being healed. The next day she was released with 100% lung capacity and drove herself to Mass that night.

A year later Lynn again was hospitalized with Histoplasmosis (a fungus). She also had a severe case of shingles along with two other bacterial infections that threatened her sight. She was in great pain but not fearful.

"Trust in Jesus and the will of God the Father," Lynn said, "kept me at peace despite the poor prognosis." After two weeks she was released from the hospital, still in great pain.

One of our lay ministers of communion, Maggie brought her communion daily. Fr. Benson gave Lynn the sacrament of the anointing of the sick, and prayed to Padre Pio for her healing.

Although Lynn recovered from this episode, several months later she had a relapse. During this bout her doctor actually ordered the nurses to make sure Lynn received the Eucharist daily.

When Lynn returned home, Maggie continued to bring communion daily. One day Maggie asked Fr. Benson to say a special mass for Lynn and her family. The Mass was offered by Fr. Benson in the Chapel where Lynn has spent hours in adoration. Padre Pio's help was invoked and Lynn said of the Mass: "I felt the presence of the Holy Spirit during this Mass. Deep down I knew I was healed." Fr. Benson also had a sense that God would heal her.

During the week of her Mass, Lynn had a special blood test to see how advanced the HIV was in her blood. The higher the viral load indicated the more imminent the threat of death by an infectious disease. "I was very anxious over the possible results since I've had HIV for thirteen years," Lynn said. "Two weeks after the test my doctor off-handedly told me my viral load report showed 'normal' like an uninfected person." He was sure it was a mistake.

The doctor called the test lab and asked for a double-check. "They insisted the blood was mine," Lynn said. "In my heart I knew I was being healed." Another test was run at a different lab. The results of this one was also normal with an even better over all reading than the first. "My doctor couldn't help but believe God is up to something good," Lynn claimed.

Lynn concluded her testimony with these words: "I do not know yet what the Lord wants me to do with my new lease on life, but I plan to follow his will in whatever way he indicated. I have surrendered to the Lord and trust fully in Jesus to guide me through what is best for me and those whose lives I touch. Praise God. Amen."

The moment Lynn completed her testimony the church erupted in applause. There was an enormous outpouring of love. I could not help but wonder what is the Holy Spirit planning for St. Margaret Mary parish.

Heal the Broken Hearted Through Intercessory Prayer

Recently one of our prayerful mothers came in to tell me the good news from Our Lady; as well as to advise me of her warning. This was the same mother who warned me last October that I would soon suffer a physical trial. A week later I was having a life threatening surgery on my aorta. Naturally, this time I paid close attention.

"Our Lady wants you to know that hundreds of thousands of souls will be touched by St. Margaret Mary community," she said. "However," this prayerful woman continued, "you are in grave danger." I believe this is why it is important to understand the gravity of listening to Our Lady when she asks you to "pray for priests." Sacred Scripture clearly warns us: "I will strike the shepherd and the sheep will be dispersed." (Mark 14:27) These words from Our Blessed Mother are also a further confirmation that intercessory prayer and the first Friday Mass of inner healing are quite important for many souls.

As I reflected on Glaucia's story of her healing of her shame and Lynn's story of her cure of AIDS, I began to ask Our Lady in prayer, "where do we go from here?" I believe her answer is "intercessory prayer is a means to evangelize."

Preparing for the Third Millennium by Intercessory Prayer

Our mass of inner healing on Friday, September 6, 1996 is to heal all of our divisions. We believe Our Blessed Mother is calling all of us to intercede with her to Jesus Christ, her son, for the union of the Body of Christ, the church. However, for this prayer of Jesus to become a reality, we must all rid ourselves of our prejudices and fears and "love one another, as he (Jesus) has loved us." Only then will the Holy Spirit heal our divisions and make us one.

Evangelization is a cry from the hearts of a wounded church. "Father make us one." That cry will be heard when each of us longs from the depths of our being to see all divisions, racial and religious, social and cultural, eliminated.

This is a great call of Pope John Paul, II in his encyclical *Ut Unum Sint* ... that they may be one. Then the year 2000, **the third millennium**, will truly be a celebration. Intercessory prayer of the church, joined with that of our mother , Mary, will touch the heart of her son, Jesus Christ and save mankind. Just as the intercession of Esther saved the Jewish people, the intercession of Mary will be heard by Jesus.

The Triumph of the Immaculate Heart of Mary is a triumph of intercession. Our meager efforts are an attempt to join with Our Lady's to plead with her son to save the world. **Jesus Christ himself is the great intercessor** before the throne of our heavenly Father. It is the heavenly Father who will send the Holy Spirit, who alone can bring about unity in the church.

At Fatima in 1917 Our Blessed Mother made us a promise. If we fasted and prayed, if we interceded with her, Jesus would hear our cry. Our world will be saved. The Triumph of the Immaculate Heart of Mary, by her intercession to her son Jesus Christ, will result in a unprecedented era of peace. Then we will be one!

We must heal the divisions in our hearts if we are to be used in this great mission of Divine Mercy.

The gospel for the sixteen Sunday in ordinary time tells it all. Jesus indicated that you cannot root up the weeds without pulling up the wheat. Divisions cannot be uprooted by programs or policies. Only the Holy Spirit can change people's hearts.

Many of my children at St. Margaret Mary have seen Jesus, Mary and Angels. Our Blessed Mother is very comfortable here. However, if we are going to succeed in intercessory prayer, we must evangelize all of the people of God. We must be certain that all of God's children, black and white, yellow and brown, young and old, rich and poor, sick and well feel comfortable in the Catholic Church. Catholics, Protestants, Jews, Communists and Atheists will all become one!

I believe the message of Our Lady to this community will take place; that this church will touch the lives of hundreds of thousands of souls. First we must rid our hearts of divisions and hatred. Only then will we be ministers of Divine Mercy. Then our prayers for church unity will be heard.

For years I have disliked charismatic healing services. I have watched headaches and stomach aches cured; and broken hearts and broken bones were untouched. If intercessory prayer is carried out in the fashion requested by Our Lady, miracles such as the healing of shame for

Glaucia and the healing of AIDS of Lynn will be an everyday occurrence. For scripture tells us: "with mighty signs and marvels, by the power of God's Spirit ... I have completed preaching the Gospel." (Romans 15:19) and that includes the injunction of Jesus: "love one another as I have loved you." When that happens, **the will of God the Father will be done here on Earth, as it id done in heaven.**

The Era of Peace

As we prepare for the coming of the third millennium the Holy Spirit is preparing St. Margaret Mary Church and all remnant communities to experience the Triumph of the Immaculate Heart of Mary through Our Lady's powerful intercession. We are being led to prepare for the return of Jesus Christ through faith in the real presence of Christ in the Eucharist. Each of you has been selected as a tool in the hands of the Holy Spirit. Divine Mercy will be your weapon in the battle against Satan. Our Lady will crush the head of the serpent through her powerful intercession. Miracles will abound, everyone will know Jesus is Alive! The Holy Spirit will usher in the great era of peace. The Remnant Churches will be models.

Let everyone reflect on the words of St. Paul in 1 Thessalonians 1:4-7:

> "We know, too, brothers beloved of God, how you were chosen. Our preaching of the gospel proved not a mere matter of words for you but one of power; it was carried on in the Holy Spirit and out of complete conviction. You know as well as we do what we proved to be like when, while still among you, we acted on your behalf. You, in turn, became imitators of us and of the Lord, receiving the word despite great trials, with the joy that comes from the Holy Spirit.

Thus you became a model for all the believers..."

[1] Pope John Paul, II, *Tertio Millennio Adveniente*, (Boston, MA.: Pauline Books & Media, 1994), page 39, #34.

[2] (Ibid, page 57, #55.)

[3] (Ibid, page 40, #34.)

[4] (Ibid, page 62, #59.)

[5] United States National Headquarters of the Marian Movement of Priests, *Our Lady speaks to her Beloved Priests* (St. Francis, Maine, 1990). Page 893, Number 532.

[6] Lynch, Daniel J., "Our Lady of Guadeloupe, The Triumph and the Great Jubilee Year 2000", *The Herald of the Reign of the Queen*, Vol. 4, No. 1, Winter 1996, 26 Lake Street, St. Alvans, Vermont 05478. Page 3

[7] The Bishops' Committee of the Confraternity of Christian Doctrine, *The New American Bible* (Nashville: Thomas Nelson Publishers, 1983), The Book of Esther Chapters 3-5.

[8] The Holy Father leaned over to bless the scapular of a child just as an assassin fire point blank at the pope. If the Holy Father had not moved, he would have been killed. After he recovered, Pope John Paul, II went to Fatima to thank Our Lady publicly for saving his life.

[9] (Pope John Paul, II, *Tertio Millennio Adveniente*, page 57, #55.)

[10] Durant, Will and Ariel, *Story of Civilization*, (New York: Simon & Schuster, 1967).

[11] (Pope John Paul, II, *Tertio Millennio Adveniente*, page 57, #55.)

[12] (Ibid, page 54, #49.)

[13] Brewer, David, "Cave Diver Finds Light in Darkness", *Huntsville Times*, (Huntsville, AL., Sun., 1996), page A-1.

Act of Consecration
of the Family to the Merciful Jesus

Almighty and Eternal Father, we, the _____ family, *(each member of the family says his first name)*, consecrate ourselves and our home to Jesus, King of Mercy.

Merciful Jesus, we proclaim You King of Mercy and enthrone Your image in our home as an act of love and trust. It is our response to Your desire that souls know You as King of Mercy and venerate Your image as the Merciful Jesus throughout the world. May it be a constant reminder of Your Love and Mercy and Your promise to work in hearts that are open to You.

Strengthen our faith, deepen our trust and increase our love for You. *Draw us* into Your Merciful Heart, the source of our healing. *Help us* to trust in Your Goodness. *Give us* the grace to live in the present moment, with patience and resignation to Your Will, not dwelling on the past or living in fear of the future.

Heal the hurts and unforgiveness that prevent us from drawing closer to You. In Your mercy, help us to *reconcile* with You and with one another. *Transform us* so that we reflect Your mercy in our family, our community and our world by our actions, words and prayers. *Sanctify us* with Your Precious Blood and refresh us with the life-giving water which flowed from Your wounded Heart.

Come Holy Spirit, *teach, guide and inspire us* in these times of doubt and confusion. Give us *courage and perseverance* in prayer. We are confident that You are always with us and our family and that through this consecration You will bring the *Peace, Healing and Reconciliation* we need in our lives.

Come, Lord Jesus, renew our hearts, restore our families.

✞✞✞✞✞

The Act of Consecration is taken from the "Rite of Enthronement of the Image of the Divine Mercy in the Home." It bears the Imprimatur of the Archdiocese of New York. For the complete enthronement ceremony and the "Nine Graces of Enthronement in the Family," by Most Rev. Emilio S. Allue, S.D.B., D.D., and Kathleen Keefe, contact:
Peace Through Divine Mercy
25 Cambridge Avenue, Yonkers, N.Y. 10707
(914) 337-0773   Fax: 914-337-7028